Leonid Ilyich
BREZHNEV

The Virgin Lands

PROGRESS PUBLISHERS

Moscow

Translated from the Russian
by Robert Daglish

Л. И. БРЕЖНЕВ

ЦЕЛИНА

На английском языке

Б $\dfrac{10202-148}{016(01)-78}$ без объявл.

1

Only let there be grain and the songs
will come of themselves, people say. And
they have good reason for saying it. Grain
has always been the staple product, the
criterion of all values. Even in our age of
great scientific and technological advance it
has remained the bedrock of the life of na-
tions. People have broken through into outer
space, they tame rivers, seas, oceans, they
extract oil and gas from the bowels of the
earth, they have mastered the energy of the
atom, but grain is still grain.

The citizens of a land with ears of grain
in its national emblem have a special, sen-
sitive and sacred attitude towards grain.
It is a feeling I, too, have known since boy-
hood.

My father was a worker, my grandfather,
a peasant, and I tried myself at both factory

and farm work. I began as a worker, but in the years of economic disruption, during long stoppages at the factory, I learned to plough, sow and reap and came to understand what it meant to grow grain with one's own hands. I became a land-use surveyor, worked in the villages of the Kursk region, in Byelorussia and in the Urals, and even later, when I was a metallurgist again, the exigencies of the time never allowed me to forget the importance of grain. Together with other Communists I went to the villages, argued it out with the kulaks at village meetings, and helped to organise the first collective farms.

One could say that only four years at the beginning of my working life were given up entirely to the countryside. But looking at it from another angle, one could also say I gave a whole four years. I began as a land-use surveyor at the very start of collectivisation and returned to the factory when the process had been basically completed. Those years, from 1927 to 1931, amounted to a whole epoch in the life of the country. When we were allotting land to the agricultural co-operatives, we realised that we were not simply breaking down the old field boundaries, but helping

the socialist reorganisation of the countryside, repatterning the whole millennial
structure of peasant life.

I say this because I feel strong ties with
both town and country, factory and field,
industry and agriculture. In Zaporozhye, as
I have already written, my main concern
was the restoration of industry, but collective farm matters demanded unremitting attention as well. In Dnepropetrovsk my time
was divided about equally between town and
country. In Moldavia, agriculture took first
place, but industry, which in that area had to
be virtually created anew, could not be left
unattended. So my concerns ran side by side,
like parallel lines, which are supposed never
to intersect, although they did in my case.

And today, too, on my desk in the
Kremlin I regularly find reports on the
course of the spring sowing, the condition
of the young crops, the rate of harvesting.
I have an old habit of calling up various
zones of the country, and when I hear comrades speaking from the Kuban, the Dnieper,
Moldavia, the Volga country or Siberia, I
can tell by their voices what kind of grain
crops they have. On the virgin lands, for
instance, if there has been no rain before
June 15, I know that several centners will

have to be deducted from the yield. If there is no rain right up till the end of the month, knock off some more. . . . At such moments, I look out of the window at Moscow and see nothing but the endless expanse of the new lands, the worried faces of the combine operators, the agronomists, the district Party Committee people and, though far away from these good friends, I again feel as if I were at their side.

The virgin lands development is part of my life. It all began on a frosty Moscow day at the end of January 1954, when I was summoned to the Central Committee of the CPSU. The problem was familiar to me already and this was not the first time I had heard about the virgin lands; the new thing was that I would be entrusted with their development on a mass scale. The project was to be launched in Kazakhstan in the coming spring and the schedule was tight. It would be a tough assignment and no one tried to hide the fact. But they also said that at that moment no task was more responsible, and that the Central Committee had decided to send P. K. Ponomarenko and me to tackle it.

The crucial factor, they told me, was that the Kazakh Republic's affairs were not in very good shape. The local leadership was working in the old way and would probably not be equal to the new tasks. To bring these virgin lands under the plough would require a different level of understanding of everything we should have to accomplish in these far-flung steppes.

Our main task was to open up the virgin lands. This, I knew, would present great difficulties. Above all, it was essential to find the right organisational solution for such a responsible task. It was not just a matter of boosting grain production in one republic but of providing a cardinal solution to the grain problem for the whole Soviet Union.

The virgin lands had to produce a grain harvest that very autumn! That autumn, without fail!

So once again, for the nth time, an abrupt change occurred in my life.

On January 30, 1954, the Presidium of the Central Committee met to discuss the situation in Kazakhstan and the tasks connected with the virgin lands project. Two days later I left by plane for Alma-Ata.

It never occurred to me then that years later I should feel the urge to tell people about that unforgettable period in my life. As at other times, I must confess, I kept no diary or notes. There were too many other things to do. But the fact is not worth regretting.

I recall the afterword that Lenin wrote to his book *The State and Revolution*. He had been going to write one more chapter but in fact he never got around to it because the October Revolution intervened. "Such an 'interruption'," he remarks with some humour, "can only be welcomed. It is more pleasant and useful to go through 'the experience of the revolution' than to write about it." Those words of Lenin's are a reminder to us all.

On the virgin lands, millions of Soviet people continued to go through the experience of the revolution and multiplied its achievements in new historical conditions. They had the vital experience of building developed socialism. So I shall always cherish the memory of those years entirely devoted to the virgin lands.

It was the first time I had ever been to Alma-Ata but I already had a warm affection for the city when I took my first look at it. It had won a place in my heart long ago. I had loved it from a distance, just as

much as I loved Kamenskoye, Dnepropetrovsk or Zaporozhye.

Like many other people serving at the
front, I had a long wait before receiving
the address to which my family had been
evacuated. In those days the first letter from
my wife with her return address on it (95,
Karl Marx St, Alma-Ata) had taken eight
long and anxious months to reach me at
the front. And it was from that letter that I
knew the names of the people who had
given shelter to my family—the Baibusynovs,
Tursun Tarabayevich and his wife Rukya
Yarulovna. I eventually found their little
house, so much like the thousands of others
in the almost entirely one-storey Alma-Ata
of those days. My wife had written to me
during the war that in summer the house
was buried in greenery and there had been
a murmuring *aryk* under the window. But
now it was February, the *aryk* had run dry
and the bare branches of the trees were
dripping in the approaching thaw. For some
reason I had a sudden vivid recall of many
of my wartime days. Should I go in? Surely
I should say thank-you to that kind Kazakh
family and bow to the walls of a house
where seven people instead of four had
managed to live happily together during

those stressful years. But I decided to wait until my wife arrived and then, if it was at all possible, go and see them together.

I continued my walk, knowing that this was the best way of forming a first impression of the city where I was to live and work. I took a look at the bazaar, which can reveal a lot to an experienced eye. It's a kind of barometer of the economic life of any locality, a mirror of the customs and traditions of its population. The Alma-Ata bazaar, noisy, crowded, kaleidoscopic, yielded a good deal of useful information and I felt intimately attracted by the whole colourful image that the city presented.

As things worked out, I lived at several different places there. My first address was out of town, at a resort about five kilometres from the now famous Medeo skating rink (it had not been built in those days). It was an extremely beautiful place. Orchards, footpaths, pure air, a babbling stream running down from the mountains. And the mountains themselves were all round us with their deep-blue shadows and glistening snowy peaks. During my last visit to Kazakhstan, in September 1976, I called at that rest home and decided to find my old room. I went up confidently to the first floor, spotted a familiar-looking door and started telling the people with me that there used to be a desk by the window and a sofa beside it.

"No, Leonid Ilyich," the housekeeper told me. "You are a whole two doors out."

This incident testifies not so much to the imperfections of human memory as to the rapidity of change. It was not just the rest home that had been reconstructed; the whole of present-day Alma-Ata is quite different from the old town. Now it is a large modern city with a population close to a million, a beautiful place with a character all its own. It is being reconstructed on a sweeping scale but according to a well thought-out plan and, I would say, lovingly. You don't see any depressing, monotonous districts. The architecture of the new developments is original and none of the major buildings repeat each other.

Whenever I pay them one of my flying visits, I say to my old friends, "Here I am again, visiting you like my own kith and kin!" When my family moved to Alma-Ata, we made our home in a small wooden peasant-type house in the same old district, known as Little Ravine. Now the house has been pulled down. Later on we moved to

Jambul Street in the centre, to an experimental house made of sandstone blocks. Apparently those blocks were not very durable because the building is no longer standing. Nor is the little cottage that sheltered my family during the war. In its place there is a large fountain, playing merrily. And only one house, on the corner of Furmanov and Kurmangazy streets, has survived to this day. But I lived there only in the last few months of my work in Alma-Ata.

At the beginning of February 1954, almost before I had time to look round the new place, I had to attend a plenary meeting of the Central Committee of the Communist Party of Kazakhstan. I must say that many of the speakers at the meeting were self-critical and outspoken. P. K. Ponomarenko and I listened attentively, but did not speak ourselves. When election time came round, a representative of the CPSU Central Committee told the plenum that the Presidium of the Central Committee recommended that Ponomarenko should be elected first secretary and Brezhnev, second secretary.

P. K. Ponomarenko and I worked in close contact, both dedicated to the same goal, sharing the many anxieties and burdens. For my part I had always valued and respected Panteleimon Kondratyevich both as the "chief partisan", who all through the war had directed the popular resistance movement operating in the enemy rear, and as a skilled organiser and a reliable comrade.

At the close of the meeting he thanked the participants and said only a few words on behalf of the two of us:

"I hope we shall be able to justify your trust. We shall work and work hard! I think that within the next two years we shall be able to report to the Central Committee that the tasks assigned to the Kazakhstan Party organisation have been fulfilled."

And indeed, exactly two years later, when I had become First Secretary of the Kazakhstan Communist Party's Central Committee, I did report to the 20th Congress of the CPSU that the Party's great task of bringing the virgin lands into cultivation had been fulfilled with honours.

2

We were all up to our eyes in work from the start. Today after so many years, looking through the documents of those days, I sometimes wonder how we managed to get so much done and all of it in time. But apparently the human organism is so built that it can adapt even to incredible strains, both nervous and physical. Again one recalls the war. The people who took part in it were stretched to the limit of human endurance. They went short of sleep and food, they got soaked in the trenches, they lay for days on end in the snow, they plunged into icy water, and yet hardly anyone suffered from colds and other "peace-time" ills. Something similar was to be observed on the virgin lands.

I have already compared the great epic of the virgin lands to a front, to a great battle won by the Party and the people. The memory of the war will always be with us, frontline men, and, after all, it's an accurate enough comparison. Of course, on the virgin lands there was no shooting, no bombing, no shelling, but all the rest was like a real battle.

To begin it, speaking in the same military terms, the first thing to do was to regroup our forces and bring up our rear, and this was no simple matter. After the plenum came the Seventh Congress of the Communist Party of Kazakhstan, which gave an analysis of the state of affairs and stated that the work of the previous Central Committee Bureau and Secretariat had been unsatisfactory.

I will explain why. In a land of very rich natural resources, with hundreds of collective farms, state farms and machine-and-tractor stations, a land where the fields were worked by tens of thousands of tractors and combines, where besides the arable land there were millions of hectares of hayfields and pastures, the production of grain, meat, cotton and wool had not increased above the pre-war level, and in some instances had actually fallen below it. The milk yields were lower than in 1940, grain crops averaged only 5 or 6 centners per hectare, cotton only 10 centners, and potatoes not more than 60 centners.

By that time even such war-devastated areas as the Kuban, the Ukraine and the Don had recovered and begun to build up their harvests and the productivity of their animal breeding. But here, although the 1953 weather had been exceptionally kind to the republic, one and a half million head of cattle were lost because of low feed stocks. During the fierce winters animals were kept in the open, without even the primitive shelter of the *koshara*. "It has always been so in our country," people would say. I should add that of the chairmen of the collective farms many had only an elementary education, and three hundred were no more than semi-literate.

Of course, there were also objective reasons for the poor state of agriculture in Kazakhstan. It reflected the neglect of this vital branch of the economy throughout the country, which was described frankly and straightforwardly by the Party at the September 1953 plenum of the CPSU Central Committee. However, even against the general background the situation in Kazakhstan looked depressing. A further difficulty was that some of the local leadership had resigned themselves to the state of affairs and acted on the principle of "we may be lucky".

"The administration of such a big republic was too much for us," Central Committee secretary I. I. Afonov, who had been directly in charge of agriculture, stated at the congress. "Instead of being in control of events, we are dashing about aimlessly like bad firemen. We merely fight the 'fires' that keep breaking out now in one place, now in another. Our basic form of administration is not even the written instruction but the instructor."

After such admissions one could scarcely wonder at the lack of initiative on the part of the regional Party committees. If anyone did try to put matters right, they did so in a rather "original" way. Aktyubinsk Region, for instance, launched a campaign for laying in a year and a half's supply of fodder. This praiseworthy object was approved and the commitment was announced in the newspapers. But any initiative, as everyone knows, should rely mainly on internal resources, on unused potentials. This is their chief value. But the Aktyubinsk people took a different course. After their

resounding promises they sent a letter to
the Council of Ministers of the Kazakh Republic: in view of this, that and the other,
for us to be able to fulfil our commitments,
you must provide us at once with three
hundred additional tractors, six thousand
tons of kerosene, so much of motor oil
and gear grease, and spare parts. In short,
help us to be heroes if you don't want
to disgrace yourselves along with us.

All my experience of administrative work –
Party, Soviet, army or economic–has long
since convinced me that the tendency to
sponge, the desire to right one's own affairs
at the expense of others, reveals as clearly
as a litmus test what this or that person is
capable of. And since we were going to
bring virgin land under cultivation and na-
tion-wide help had been promised, such
sponging could assume dangerous propor-
tions. So I resolved to take special note of
this phenomenon.

I have often spoken of the need to look
after one's cadres. I have in mind, of course,
people who have shown that they know how
to work. It is not a matter of being all-
forgiving: the incompetent and dishonest
must be resolutely replaced. Here I could
see for myself that some of the leaders at

various levels were often promoted on the basis of cronyism. This had to be stamped out at once, and P. K. Ponomarenko and myself took a tough stand. So that there should be no misunderstandings, we announced the fact openly and straightforwardly. In one of my first speeches (before the electorate in Alma-Ata in March 1954) I said:

"In view of the enormous tasks now confronting the Kazakhstan Party organisation the importance of correct cadre policy has immeasurably increased. The Seventh Congress of the Kazakhstan Communist Party has revealed serious shortcomings and mistakes in cadre policy work, which show that some leaders have lost their sense of responsibility and selected personnel not according to their abilities, but on the principle of personal attachment. We cannot tolerate this. The republic has plenty of mature, experienced people, well qualified for promotion to positions of leadership and capable of performing the tasks set by the Party."

So we went on selecting strong-willed leaders and bringing up our rear services, while waiting impatiently for the Party's decision to start opening up the virgin lands.

2*

And at the very end of February 1954 came
the historic February-March plenum of the
CPSU Central Committee, which passed the
decision "On Further Increase of the Country's Grain Production and Cultivation of
Virgin and Abandoned Lands".

The great battle in the Kazakh steppes
began. It was spread over a huge geograph-
ical area. Northern Kazakhstan extends
1,300 kilometres from East to West and
900 kilometres from North to South. The
total area of its present six regions (there
used to be five)—Kustanai, Tselinograd (for-
merly Akmolinsk), North-Kazakhstan, Kokchetav, Turgai and Pavlodar—exceeds 600,000
square kilometres, much more than the
whole territory of, say, France. And over
this huge area we had to plough up 250,000
square kilometres of fertile steppeland, an
area larger than the whole of Britain.

Besides us, Altai Territory, Krasnoyarsk
Territory, Novosibirsk and Omsk Regions,
the Volga country, the Urals and the Far
East were also involved in the virgin lands
project. As many people will recall, the area
of virgin and abandoned lands brought
under cultivation in the USSR now totals
42 million hectares, 25 million of which
were ploughed in Kazakhstan. And 18 mil-

lion of that total were opened up in the Kazakhstan steppes in 1954 and 1955.

These figures are striking, but the development of the virgin lands was not just a matter of ploughing. It meant housing, schools, hospitals, kindergartens, creches, recreation centres and new roads, bridges, airfields and animal farms, grain elevators, storehouses, factories. In short, everything that people need to live a normal life and for modern farming.

I cannot give a detailed, day-by-day account of events. A good deal has already been written about the virgin lands project, the difficulties of its development, and about the lives and achievements of its pioneers. I will describe only the main lines of our activity, the strategy and tactics that we adopted to make the virgin lands what they have become today; regulation of the use of land on the new farms and the old ones that had been expanded; selection of sites for the centres of the new state farms; the reception and accommodation of hundreds of thousands of volunteers in country that was as yet totally unprepared for human habitation; the urgent building of tens and, later, hundreds of state farm settlements; the selection of many thousands of specialists; the building of close-knit harmonious collectives out of a heterogeneous mass of people; and the actual ploughing of the virgin soil and first spring sowing.... And this had to be done not in consecutive order but all at once, simultaneously.

To give the reader an idea, for example, of the scale of the work to strengthen the local leadership, which had to be done in a very short time, I will say that in 1954 alone we considered and recommended for work on the virgin lands more than five hundred new secretaries of district Party Committees and secretaries of primary Party organisations, thousands of collective-farm chairmen, agronomists, animal specialists, engineers and mechanics. They included a good many splendid local functionaries, and even more newcomers. The CPSU Central Committee, the Union ministries, and many republics and regions who generously shared their cadres with the virgin lands were a tremendous help to us.

The Ministry of State Farms of the USSR set up a special headquarters for selecting personnel. Its offices reminded one of a railway station, there were so many people coming and going. I went to that headquarters and for weeks on end sat there from early morning till midnight interviewing candidates. I never grudged the time needed for a detailed and thorough talk with anyone who intended to go out to the virgin lands. It was important that everybody should realise the complexity and depth of the plan, acquire real faith in it and serve it to the very best of his strength and ability. In the course of these conversations I would try to find out whether the person had a real desire to go, what experience he had, how healthy he was, and whether his family was prepared to move out there as well. The questions I was asked in return were no less numerous: when to go, how much land had this or that state farm, what kind of soil, where would the other people be from, how much machinery and equipment was being assigned there, what to take for a start and so on.

On the spot, in the corridors of the ministry, between interviews the future directors would recruit their specialists. This was how the famous quintettes were formed: director, chief agronomist, chief engineer, construction engineer, and chief accountant. Later we went over to sextettes instead of quintettes, including in the package a deputy director for administrative matters. Experience showed that without such a manager it was difficult to cope with the vital problem of providing normal living facilities and amenities.

In my office at the Central Committee I had a big map of Kazakhstan on the wall. Just as in the old days at the front I used to mark the positions of army units, their zones of operation and lines of attack, so would I now mark on this map the deployment of hundreds of farms and operational centres. Circles indicated the main bases from which the offensive was to be launched: the towns nearest to the areas of cultivation, stations, and settlements lost in the boundless expanses of the steppe. Green-and-red flags indicated the old collective and state farms, which had also considerably expanded their crop area by driving into the virgin lands. And there were also red flags for the centres of the new state farms, which were then still to be built. In 1954, ninety red flags appeared on the map. By the beginning of 1956 there were 337!

People usually write in their memoirs how the directors of the state farms and their main specialists would drive out into the steppe with nothing but the order of their appointment, a bank account number and a rubber stamp in their pockets. They would arrive at their destination, drive some stakes in the ground for the name-board of the farm, and begin operations. . . . It's quite true that this is how things were done. But many of my old acquaintances, while paying tribute to the romantic side, forget one essential detail: they drove their stakes into the ground not at random, but at a strictly designated spot. And besides the orders and rubber stamps in their pockets, the state farm directors also had briefcases that contained maps showing the kinds of lands allocated to the new farms and how they were to be used. There was romanticism galore on the virgin lands, and as many difficulties. But the situation should not be oversimplified, as if people just roamed out into the steppe and started ploughing away with plenty of land all round to choose from.

Construction engineers have a concept—the zero cycle. It means the works connected with siting the building, the laying out of its foundations and underground communications. This is a big, though outwardly unimpressive, job that has to be done before any building can be erected. In agriculture the "zero cycle", figuratively speaking, is the land-use surveying, all the work involved in allocating land to its various purposes. Land-use surveying provides a kind of general plan determining the outlines and character of the farm, the location and size of its fields, meadows and pastures, the siting of its buildings, its water supplies, and much else of vital importance for life and production.

At the republic's Party Central Committee an operational working group for the virgin lands took shape more or less automatically in the very first days. Later it was variously named: working, operational, some even called it the republic's virgin lands headquarters. Its activities were indeed reminiscent of a wartime headquarters. I was in charge of it. This group was not set up officially, it had no specially appointed members. All the people in it held their usual posts, but they were all directly connected with agriculture. Besides myself, the group included Fazil Karibzhanovich Karibzhanov, the Kazakhstan CC secretary for agriculture, Andrei Konstantinovich Morozov and Vasily Andreyevich Liventsov, heads of the agricultural and state farm departments of the Central Committee, Grigory Andreyevich Melnik, the republic's Minister of Agri-

culture, Mikhail Dmitriyevich Vlasenko, the
Minister of State Farms, and a number of
other top officials. Of course, hundreds and
hundreds of people came to the republic's
Central Committee on matters connected
with the virgin lands, but the comrades I
have named were the high command, the
people who directed the whole enormous
operation.

The allocation of land for ploughing was
an urgent matter and unprecedented in
scale. And if one had to say who was the
first to go out into those boundless steppes,
the answer would be that it was the scientists, the hydro-engineers, the botanists, the
land-use surveyors, the agronomists. They
are the people who, I feel, deserve first
praise.

The fertile lands were not all located
together. They had to be found, assessed,
delimited. It had to be decided which of
them were suitable for grain, and which
for meadows and pastures. Nearly one-third
of the territory of Kazakhstan—100 million
hectares—had to be studied by the land-use
surveyors. The Kazakh Republic's Academy
of Sciences alone made up and sent out into
the steppe 69 combined expeditions and
groups. Specialists from academies, insti-

tutes and experimental stations all over the
country took part in studying and assessing
the land. Thousands of soil scientists, botanists, hydro-engineers, land-use surveyors,
and agronomists from Russia, Kazakhstan,
the Ukraine and Byelorussia studied 178 districts of the republic and for a start found
22.6 million hectares of land fit for the
plough. These lands, in the form of detailed
maps of the soil, their vegetation cover and
with strictly marked water supplies and raw
material resources for the production of local
building materials, were submitted by them
first to the district, and then to the regional
and republican agencies.

I had a land-use surveyor's diploma. So
both in my capacity as Central Committee
secretary of such a large republic and as a
specialist in land surveying I was extremely
interested in all this. The scientists helped
us to get our bearings quickly, identified six
clearly defined natural-economic zones on
the territory of the republic, and gave clear
recommendations on where grain should be
sown, where animal breeding should be pur-
sued, where the two should be combined,
and where irrigated farming should be developed.

At that time I made many pleasant acquaintanceships with the Kazakhstan comrades. I had taken a liking to the Kazakhs back in my wartime days. They were very thorough, unassuming, dutiful and brave soldiers and officers. In the lulls between the fighting they were always yearning for their homeland, for the spacious steppes with their waving feather grass. Sometimes when I heard a Kazakh singing one of his melodious and mournful songs, I would go up to him and ask, "What are you singing about?"

"About the steppe. About the herd. I remembered my girl. . . ."

"A man can miss his girl and miss his home, but the steppe. . . . You have the Ukrainian steppe here. Isn't it just as good?"

"Yes, it's as good. Only our steppe is quite different."

And now, years later, I rejoice to see what fine Soviet cadres of Kazakh nationality have developed. Among them are top Party and managerial personnel, outstanding scientists, gifted specialists in all fields, including culture and the arts.

I must say that the Kazakhs as a whole, the overwhelming majority, greeted the Party's decision to plough the feather grass steppes with tremendous enthusiasm and approval. For the Kazakhs the cultivation of the virgin lands presented a complex problem. For centuries the Kazakh people had been involved in animal breeding and now large numbers of them would have to break down the whole previous pattern of life in the steppes, become crop farmers, farm-machine operators, specialists in grain growing. But the local people had the wisdom and courage to take a most active and heroic part in the opening up of the virgin lands. The Kazakh people rose to the demands of history. They understood the needs of the whole country and showed their revolutionary, internationalist qualities.

My friendship with Dinmukhamed Akhmedovich Kunayev has lasted for nearly a quarter of a century. In those days he was president of the Kazakh Republic's Academy of Sciences and, naturally enough, we got to know each other in the very first days of my stay in Alma-Ata. Educated as a mining engineer, a specialist in non-ferrous metals, he was not a man of narrow interests. He had a statesmanlike mind, could think broadly and boldly, and expressed some original and profound ideas about the huge resources and prospects of Kazakhstan. This calm, considerate, charming man also possessed a strong will and belief in Party principle. Soon he became chairman of the republic's Council of Ministers. Today he heads the Kazakhstan Party organisation and is a member of the Politbureau of the CPSU Central Committee.

Dimash Akhmedovich (the friendly form of address adopted by everybody; no one uses his full name—Dinmukhamed) recommended to me as a consultant on the virgin lands the director of the Institute of Soil Science, Umirbek Uspanovich Uspanov. Under the direction of this hard-working scientist the institute had accumulated vast information on the soil characteristics of Kazakhstan, and its members made a considerable contribution to everything concerning the deployment of the new state farms.

I also have pleasant memories of Vasily Alexandrovich Sheremetyev, head of the land-use surveying department of the republic's Ministry of Agriculture. He was a unique person. Winter and summer he went about without a hat, in a soldier's tunic, topboots and always with an army-type field bag slung over his shoulder. During the long years of his work in Kazakhstan he had walked the length and breadth of the

country and knew the steppes blindfold. He
was absolutely indispensable when it came
to choosing the sites for the central buildings of the state farms. His field bag struck
me as a regular treasure trove such as one
reads about in fairy-tales: from it he would
produce maps, diagrams, notepads with the
names of hundreds of streams, landmarks,
mountains, sheltered spots, and also many
of the names of local inhabitants, people
who really knew the land. He always insisted on including them in any commission
for setting up new farms, and these old
Kazakh *aksakals* would gladly help us.

On learning that I had some experience
of land-use surveying Sheremetyev was absolutely delighted and began treating me as
a colleague and sometimes even abused the
fact by demanding my intervention in
minor matters that could have been decided
without me. But quite often intervention was
needed. And it had to be serious. One day
he burst into my office excitedly with an
armful of land-use survey maps that had
been sent to him, if I remember, from Kokchetav Region.

"Look what they're doing! They've tacked
new areas on to the old lands without any
characterisation of the fields. I ring up the

district centre and get indignant and they calmly reply: what's all the fuss about? It's not our first year's ploughing. As soon as spring comes, the snow will go away and we'll see at once where we ought to plough."

He was talking about the collective farms that had been allocated new lands for cultivation. The people there had been working in the steppe for years and naturally considered themselves too knowledgeable to be interfered with. This psychology had to be overcome. We had to combat the oversimplified approach and demand that the selection of virgin lands was always carried out on a strictly scientific basis.

Not only did one have to be able to take immediate action; one also had to go deep into things and plan for the future. One could not grudge time or strength for the accomplishment of such a splendid goal. Quite often I would stay on at the Central Committee late into the night, again and again examining the maps and specifications of dozens of farms before they were finally accepted by decision of the Council of Ministers of the republic and by order of the Ministry of Agriculture of the USSR.

It is well known that 1954, if one takes into consideration the considerable doubts that some people had, brought tremendous success in the cultivation of the virgin lands. Instead of 13 million hectares for the country as a whole, 19 million hectares came under the plough. And Kazakhstan also overfulfilled its cultivation plan. Need one say how greatly this inspired people and buttressed their confidence in the project. Having analysed our first experience and weighed the country's potential, the CPSU Central Committee and the USSR Council of Ministers passed a new decision "On Further Cultivation of the Virgin and Abandoned Lands to Increase Grain Production". Kazakhstan was given the task of setting up an additional 250 new state farms.

The first ninety state farms founded in 1954 had been sited on the more convenient lands, comparatively close to the railways and the available rivers. Now we had to drive deep into those boundless steppes. Our assignments became even more complicated. For one thing it was more difficult to select land for ploughing. This gave rise to contradictions or, if you like, conflicting points of view.

I recall the battles that we had over two regions. The USSR Ministry of Agriculture held that nothing at all should be ploughed up in Aktyubinsk Region because the land there was supposed to be unsuitable for growing grain. On the other hand, when the local comrades in Karaganda Region proposed setting up eighteen state farms on unproductive land, their "initiative" was unreservedly supported. I called the minister in Moscow and said that this was an obvious mistake, but he described the Karaganda people as patriots and pace-setters and at the same time, evidently in the heat of the moment, accused the leaders of the northern regions, where the reserves of virgin land were indeed rather small, of conservatism and other mortal sins.

Such verbal polemics, without figures, reasons and arguments, are quite useless. I flew out to Aktyubinsk Region, met the specialists there, and saw for myself that there were some fertile lands in the region. I insisted on a combined expedition of scientists being sent there immediately. They did their work thoroughly and honestly and discovered 1.7 million hectares of good ploughland. A visit to Karaganda also convinced me that we were right. Once again I was confirmed in my belief that agriculture demands a scientific, not voluntarist approach.

3*

In Alma-Ata we held a meeting of the republic's regional Party Committee secretaries and regional Executive Committee chairmen. The Central Committee of the Communist Party of Kazakhstan specially brought up for discussion the results of the selection of lands for the new state farms. In a concluding speech I said at the time (I quote from the minutes):

"We have done a tremendous amount of work on allocating lands. Nearly 9 million hectares have been found and delimited. But the work is not yet finished. On these grounds—in both the figurative and literal senses—arguments have arisen with the Ministry of Agriculture that at present we do not intend to abandon. We shall stick to our positions and we hope to defend them. It seems to us that Karaganda has not yet sorted out its land resources. It has been proposed that 18 state farms should be organised. This seems quite a lot. But the plan for their deployment cannot be supported, because unsuitable lands have been chosen. At the same time, in a number of districts of the region that I have visited myself there are good lands where state farms should be built."

I write in such detail about the surveying of the steppe and the allocation of sites for the new farms because the "zero cycle" in cultivation of the virgin lands was of tremendous importance. The fate of the land that was to be ploughed and the whole future life there depended on it.

The first spring season on the virgin lands left various impressions on my memory— joy, triumph, intense strain, difficulties. The steppe turned out to be a tough nut to crack, tougher than it had seemed at first. Not only was the centuries-old sward with its tangle of wirelike roots so firmly packed that it would scarcely yield to the plough; another difficulty arose from the fact that on the Kazakh virgin lands there is practically no spring in the usual sense of the word. Winter almost immediately turns into summer. Fierce heat marches literally in the wake of the melting snows, in May there is practically no rain, the land dries out quickly and becomes rock-hard and doubly difficult to plough.

The first furrows everywhere were cut with great celebrations and meetings. The

first squares were also ploughed successfully. On the virgin lands these were un-
usual. Everywhere the surveyors gave the
tractor teams equal portions of untouched
steppe, two kilometres square, in other
words, an area of 400 hectares.

"That's a nice little square for you, plenty of room to move in!" the tractor drivers
would joke. "Just switch on your engine and
keep going till your fuel runs out."

But soon they found that they had to stop
more and more often. The engines stalled,
the ploughshares broke, the frames bent.
Only a leviathan like the S-80 could pull a
five-bottom plough. The manoeuvrable but
light-weight DT-54 and NATI were not
powerful enough for the virgin lands. Everywhere people began taking one or even two
shares off their ploughs. This not only reduced their performance; it threatened the
whole plan for cultivation of the virgin
lands.

The pre-sowing treatment of the virgin
soil was not an easy business either. It had
to be gone over several times with disk
ploughs, then with duck-foot cultivators,
then it had to be harrowed and rolled with
water-filling rollers. And only after that
could the seeders be sent into action, al-

though the interval between the first breaking of the soil and sowing could not be more than four or five days. We knew that otherwise the soil would dry out and it would be useless to sow it.

I remember my first trip to the sowing, in Kustanai Region. N. S. Khrushchov had arrived. He was at the station of Tobol. Soon a big conference took place there. It was held at the Maikul Stud Farm, which was also turning up virgin land. We all assembled in the farm director's office—P. K. Ponomarenko, myself, I. P. Khramkov, first secretary of the Kustanai Regional Party Committee, I. G. Slazhnev, chairman of the Regional Executive Committee, M. G. Motoriko, director of the Kustanai Stud Farm (now Kazakhstan's Minister of Agriculture), scientists of the All-Union Institute of Mechanisation of Agriculture, and others. There was much to discuss, but the key problem was the turning of the furrow slice.

We had had a lot of trouble with it. The ordinary plough would not lay the massive slice of sward cut by the coulters at the bottom of the furrow. The broken sward stuck out at all angles and did not get covered by the lumpy lower soil. Such a field was very awkward to disk. We decided to adjourn the conference and go and see what all this looked like in practice and drove out to one of the tractor teams.

The tractor drivers were jumpy, the work was going badly. No matter how they tried, the slice would not turn over completely. I went up to them, joined in the conversation and asked what they thought could be done. They replied that the existing ploughs were no good. A different kind was needed.

"What kind?"

"We've been saying it for a long time, but what's the use!" one of the drivers exclaimed. "You've got to organise production of ploughs with helical and semi-helical mould-boards. And it must be done at once."

I must say that when N. S. Khrushchov realised what the matter was he became very cross and hurled some sharp accusations at the scientists. Why hadn't they foreseen this? Surely there had been time to advise the factories about such ploughs? Action was taken and within a month the first of the new ploughs began arriving on the virgin lands.

But this was only after a month. The ploughing of the virgin lands was already in full swing and we had to think of a way of keeping up the pace that had been set.

One evening I made my usual round of telephone calls to the state farms to find out how much had been ploughed and what difficulties they were having. I also rang the Orjonikidze State Farm. Its director, F. P. Kukhtin, said that things were going well, but asked us to send him some spare ploughshares.

"The shares don't last five minutes. . . . But we're ploughing at full speed. Come and see for yourself."

I asked how the sward turned over into the furrow. "Fine," came the answer. "We're tucking it in like a baby."

The next morning a big party of us went out to the Orjonikidze Farm. S. V. Kalchenko, the Deputy Minister of State Farms of the USSR, joined us and at the district centre we picked up M. G. Roginets, a CPSU Central Committee representative on the virgin lands. I had known Mikhail Georgievich since my days in the Ukraine, where he had been first secretary of the Chernigov Regional Party Committee, just at the time when I was working in Dnepropetrovsk. I hadn't seen him since then and I was glad at this unexpected meeting. Subsequently, as first secretary of the Kokchetav Regional Party Committee, and later, as Minister of

State Farms and Minister of Agriculture of
the Kazakh Republic, he put a lot of work
into developing the virgin lands.

During the journey to the Orjonikidze
State Farm it transpired that it was he who
had suggested "one little thing" and the
ploughing of the virgin lands in the districts
under his charge was going well. The scene
in the fields was encouraging. The tractor
drivers were easily keeping up a normal
speed and the ploughs were biting into the
virgin soil with a pleasingly steady crunch
and tear. How so?

"I said it was just a little thing," Roginets replied with a smile. "We take off only
a thin layer of sward, just the top. Look,
the coulters are angled to a depth of only
seven centimetres, not to eleven as stated
in the instructions. That's how we manage
it."

And sure enough, the coulters, as we then
noticed, were cutting off a thin slice of
sward, like the rind off a piece of fatback,
and tossing it, grassy side down, to the bottom of the furrow. They really were "tucking it in like a baby". I felt I had to reproach
Mikhail Georgievich and the comrades from
the farm. Why had they kept quiet about
it?

"Well, you could hardly make a hullabaloo over a little thing like that. I thought people would think of it themselves. It's not all that hard," Roginets replied.

"You thought of it," I said, "but you mustn't forget that the whole country has come to the virgin lands and a lot of them are young people. Everything useful that's been learnt by experience must be spread around quickly. Even some of the experienced ones may have thought of it but would be afraid to take the responsibility of infringing instructions. That's so, isn't it, Stepan Vlasyevich?"

"Yes, they might be afraid," Kalchenko responded.

"So send out an instruction. Wherever they're having trouble with the sward, let them angle their coulters at seven centimetres instead of eleven."

"I'll write it today."

All the way back, we kept pulling Mikhail Georgievich's leg, telling him that a Ukrainian always likes to rip off as thick a slice of fatback as he can, but he only took a thin one. We had never seen such a thing before.

A day later there was a meeting of the bureau of the Kustanai Regional Party Committee. Among other matters the question of building roads on the virgin lands was discussed. The majority was in favour of highways, for motor transport. It might be dearer and take longer, but it would be better to start at once developing a fundamental, modern road network with an eye to the long-term prospects. Large grain elevators were to be built simultaneously at the main junctions. N. S. Khrushchov, however, maintained that it would be more expedient to build several narrow-gauge railways, to which, so he claimed, the grain could be brought up from the way-out districts. No arguments against this idea were taken into consideration. So a narrow-gauge line from Kustanai to Uritskoye was laid, and then another, from Yesil to Turgai. This was a mistake. Neither of the lines came up to expectations as a means of transporting grain and both were soon dismantled.

I cite this fact not in order to show that a Party and state functionary must at the same time be a transport expert, an economist, an engineer and so on. He need not be all these things, but he must master the laws of general development and also rely on concrete scientific and practical knowledge. And in any event he should never

regard himself as the sole and incontrovertible authority in all fields of human en-
deavour.

Modern economics, politics, the life of society are so complex that they will yield
only to powerful collective reasoning. One
must listen to all that the experts and
scientists have to say, and not only to those
of one trend or school. One must be able
to consult the people, so as to avoid
any "chopping and changing", hasty, ill-
considered, voluntaristic decisions. These
are particularly dangerous when a whole geo-
graphical area is being developed economically, socially and culturally, when it is a
matter of the long-term policies to be adopted there, and of being able to see far ahead.

From Kustanai I set out on a trip round
the virgin land regions, districts and state
farms, where sowing was everywhere in
progress.

At the stations of Yesil and Atbasar I
encountered what was literally babel. Their
capacity was in no way equal to the amount
of freight that was arriving. Even in those
days Yesil was known as the gateway to the
virgin lands, although it was only a tiny
little station amid the vastness of the steppes.
Massive quantities of freight were also

arriving at the district centre of Atbasar.
The old dusty little township, open to every
wind that blew, with its squat dwellings and
stunted vegetation was receiving trains
loaded with machinery, timber, cement, prefabricated housing, field-camp wagons,
metal, petrol, seed, food and merchandise,
and not only for its own virgin land farms,
but for the three adjoining districts too. The
whole population of the town had been mo-
bilised to get the trains unloaded.

Members of the district Party Committee
bureau, functionaries of the district Executive Committee, and YCL activists were on
duty round the clock at the station, meeting
the trains, directing the unloading, receiving
the newcomers and trying to billet them in
the homes of the local people. I say "trying" because the new arrivals did not want
to be held up for a minute. They were eager
to get out into the steppe and would go
around shouting amid the general uproar the
names of their farms: "Marinovsky! At-
basarsky! Dnepropetrovsky! Baumansky!"
It had to be explained to them that the first
parties had already been sent to the state
farms, that they were already ploughing and
sowing out there and building accommodation for the reinforcements. Until there was

somewhere to live, it was no use sending
any more newcomers. We also explained
that the rivers were in spate and to make
the journey now would be simply dangerous. But arguments were of no avail. Pla-
cards were waved above the heads of the
milling crowds: "All for the State Farm!"
"Up the Virgin Lands!"

To the farms situated, like Atbasar, on the
right bank of the River Ishim machinery
and people were still being dispatched in
tractor and truck convoys. But some of the
machinery, earmarked for the left-bank half
of the district, was held up by the spring
floods. It would have been a sin to leave it
standing idle and the local authorities decided to use it temporarily in the right-bank
collective and state farms and machine-and-
tractor stations. But suddenly one of the
tractor teams disappeared.

It turned out that the leader of the team,
Vladimir Chekalin, having heard about this
decision, had roused his lads during the
night and gone off with the tractors. These
lads were bound for the Red Dawn Collective Farm on a Komsomol assignment.
They had formed themselves into a team
when still at their point of departure and
were travelling with their tractors. Vasily

Filippovich Makarin, the district Party secretary, set out in pursuit of the "runaways". On the bank of the Ishim he discovered some tractors and Chekalin himself, all alone.

"Where are the other go-it-aloners?"

"They'll be here in a minute."

"Who gave you permission to break discipline like this?"

"We're not breaking discipline. Who are the tractors intended for? The Red Dawn Collective Farm. And that's where they're going to turn up the virgin lands, as per instructions. We'll find a ford!"

Try as he would, the Party secretary could not make the team-leader see reason. He was adamant. Meanwhile the other tractor drivers came up to the bank of the river. Among them were some white beards to be seen—the local *aksakals*. When he heard what the argument was about, one of the old men turned to Makarin.

"Ah, secretary, why are you scolding the youngster? It's your own fault! Why didn't you send the machines beforehand? Didn't you know there would be a big flood after all that snow?"

The Kazakhs showed the lads where the ford was and told them that at that spot the bed of the river was solid rock. The drivers soon dragged their tractors over to the other bank and put them to work in the collective farm the same day. The same ford was then used to send machinery across to the other state farms on the left bank, the Dnepropetrovsky, Marinovsky, and Baumansky.

Makarin was still excited and upset when he told me about this. After all, there had been an element of risk. And he was angry about the breach of discipline. But there had also been persistence, resourcefulness and daring. Incidentally, after the episode of the "runaways" a makeshift crossing was arranged. The people of Atbasar launched all their boats and two ferries were put together and spring and summer they carried people, trucks, machinery, fuel and food across the river. This was also an example of true frontline resourcefulness. And I encountered so many such examples on the virgin lands in those years that I could not possibly tell about them all here.

From Atbasar I drove on with Makarin. We took our time, visiting one farm after another, going from team to team. It was the first I had seen of the Kazakh steppe in the spring and I delighted in it. What an expanse! Even the sun must tire by the time it travelled from one horizon to the other. The vernal steppe was a blaze of colour. The blue gleams of the floodwater. The fresh fragrant grass glistening in the sunshine. The flowering tulips. And here and there, all the way across this great sweep of green lay the black squares of land ploughed for the first time.

But on that wonderful sunny day I was beset by a worrying thought. In the course of my observations I had noticed that the squares of newly ploughed land were not being sown. The seeders were at work only on the old ploughland. I recall local people telling me that it had always been so; they sowed only in the second year. I did not hurry to ask questions. Only in one team did I ask a local man, not a newly arrived tractor driver, "When are you going to sow the virgin land? In June?"

"Sow in June?" he repeated in surprise. "We'd be a laughing stock. We have a saying down here: you might as well spit at a dune as sow in June."

Makarin was silent on the way back to Atbasar.

"Isn't it time you made a report?" I said.

"What is there to report? You've seen for yourself."

It turned out that no one intended to sow this spring in Atbasar District. Why? Makarin explained: it was an old custom that any newly ploughed land should be sowed only the following spring because it was always ploughed late, never before June. But why late? Because before this the peasant was busy with his sowing. He couldn't manage both jobs at once, sowing and ploughing. And by the time he got around to the virgin land there was no sense in sowing. The earth waited for the next spring and only then did it yield its first and usually good harvest. Hence the long-standing traditions, the accepted notions and ingrained prejudices. The Atbasar people had debated the matter at great length and decided not to sow in the first year.

I must admit that much had been said about this before. Behind me I had the advice of serious scientists. I had been through heaps of material provided by expeditions that had begun to investigate the virgin lands long ago. I shall have more to say about that later. For the future, 1955 harvest we planned to plough up as much land as possible precisely in June because late summer or autumn ploughing both of virgin land and underwinter fallow was just as undesirable in these parts as June sowing. This had been proved by scientists and provided for in our plans. But in that first spring we were ploughing virgin land in April and May, and not for the next year's harvest, but for this year's!

People would have to be persuaded. We drove back to town, each thinking his own thoughts. I had supper with Makarin at his home. We drank two glasses with the Siberian meat dumplings, a favourite dish of mine, prepared by his wife Feodosia Kuzminichna: one to a successful beginning on the virgin lands, and the other to our hostess. That evening Vasily Filippovich was tireless in asking all kinds of questions.

"Are you really convinced that these lands will become one of the country's biggest granaries?"

"So you doubt it, do you?"

"We've had such a struggle with this land. . . ."

"I'm not only convinced, Vasily Filippovich, I am proud to be involved in the project."

I understood this man well, I knew his state of mind. He was one of the old local functionaries that we, despite the radically changed scale of work, had decided to keep on at his former post. And we had not been mistaken. The great events had only at first put them rather at a loss. Makarin was one of thousands of district Party Committee secretaries, those great workers who carry the main burden of the most difficult Party work, the work at grass-roots level. He had been living and working in one of the quietest little towns you can imagine, buried in the remote sun-scorched steppe, and his life had rolled by at a gentle, steady pace. But then came the year 1954 and the town became the epicentre of the virgin lands campaign, and in full view of the whole country. To Makarin's credit it can be said that he possessed that peasant thoroughness and the kind of mind that gets to the bottom of things and enables a man to acquire a deep faith in a new cause and to give himself up to it entirely with all the remarkable strength of his talent.

The next morning, at my request he assembled state farm directors A. V. Zaudalov, I. G. Likhobaba and G. Y. Tutikov at the district Party Committee office. The chairman of the district Executive Committee S. K. Galushchak, his deputy Rakhim

Kaisarin and other comrades also attended. Once again we discussed everything, I listened attentively to everyone's opinion, and in conclusion I said:

"It's a good thing that you are taking a thorough and cautious attitude to this great project. But let's go into what the argument is really about. Could the private peasant farmer, even if he was, as they say, in good fettle, work the virgin land quickly, as we can now? Of course, not! With a wooden plough or, at best, a drill plough he could plough up his own patch of land even in May, but he simply didn't have the means to cultivate it. So he would wait for nearly a year, or even more, until the sods crumbled by themselves under the influence of sun, water and frost. Should we take this peasant as our standard and borrow his bitter and inescapable experience? I think not. With the machinery we have today we can make the upturned soil soft, porous and ready to receive the seed within two or three days. And we can reap the reward of our labours the very same year. So decide for yourselves what is the best thing to do."

"What is there to decide? I've been saying for a long time we ought to sow!" Zaudalov responded warmly.

"Well, sow then."

"You see, it's not that anyone's preventing us or forbidding us. What they say is: mind you don't come a cropper. You're not a local man, you don't know this soil. And that's bound to put doubts into your head."

"We'll sow everything we've ploughed to date," Makarin assured me. "You've convinced us. It looks as if we thought ourselves into a muddle."

"All right then, but remember another thing," I added. "The arguments that were brought up here were agronomic and technical, and nothing was said about the political side of the question. But what we also have to consider is not just the feasibility but the necessity of sowing this spring and not later. And it's not only an economic necessity. It's a matter of politics. Let the whole world know once again that we, Communists, can accomplish great things in a very short space of time. And besides, it is important from the human angle that every cultivator of the virgin lands should see the fruits of his labour this year."

4

Sometimes people ask who fathered the idea of cultivating the virgin lands. I maintain that this question is wrong in itself, that it implies an attempt to attribute an outstanding achievement of our Party and people to the "vision" and will of one man.

The opening up of the virgin lands was a splendid idea conceived by the Communist Party, the realisation of which helped almost instantly, if one thinks in terms of history, to turn the country's lifeless, remote but fertile eastern steppes into a land with a developed economy and flourishing culture.

The settlement of the vast expanses of Kazakhstan, Western Siberia and Russia's Far East by impoverished peasants from European Russia began, as we know, in the nineteenth century. It received a big boost with the opening of the Great Trans-Siberian Railway. But we also know what happened later. Millions of the dispossessed, landless, starving peasants of tsarist Russia headed eastwards with their families to the "promised land" in the desperate hope of finding land and happiness there. They travelled in crowded goods vans, two-wheeled carts and wagons. Thousands of these would-be settlers died on the road, exhausted by the long arduous journey, hunger and disease. Art and history have left us many testimonies to that dramatic epic. Take, for instance, the painting *Death of a Settler* by Sergei Ivanov. Way out in the remote steppe, on the road to a destination he will never reach, the head of a peasant family, its bread-winner, dies. What will happen to his widow, to the children? This is the painful question we usually ask ourselves when viewing that famous painting.

But even those who arrived safely on those lands that had never known the plough found themselves in desperate straits. They entered into single combat with the wild and rigorous steppe. There was nowhere to live, no roads, no water, no help from anywhere. A skinny nag with a wooden or at best an iron plough were all the "technical means" they had.

The "opening up of the virgin lands" in pre-revolutionary times assumed the magnitude of a national disaster. The heartless, inhuman attitude of the tsarist authorities to the settlers was indignantly described by Chekhov, Korolenko and Uspensky. In his essays called *Travels to the Settlers* Gleb Uspensky painted a typical picture of what he saw in one of the farmsteads.

"Black heaps of something that looked like piled peat or dried dung, not very large, scattered here and there suggest nothing that bears the slightest resemblance to human habitation; not a single human creature anywhere to be seen, and not the slightest possibility of imagining that people could live here. And yet live they do...."

We encountered the ruins of such "black heaps"–earthen dwellings–here and there in the steppe and they always evoked sad thoughts about the misfortunes of those first settlers on the virgin lands.

In the face of such unbearable conditions the peasants took flight back to Russia, to the Ukraine and Byelorussia–into the arms of a no less bitter fate. With fierce anger Lenin branded the policy of the tsarist government towards the settlers. He wrote:

"It is the poorest who return to Russia, the most unfortunate, who have lost everything and are bitterly angry. The land question must have become very acute in Siberia for it to have become impossible, despite the desperate efforts of the government, to accommodate hundreds of thousands of settlers." And in another article: "This gigantic wave of returning settlers reveals the desperate plight, ruin and destitution of the peasants who sold everything at home in order to go to Siberia, and who are now forced to come back from Siberia completely ruined and pauperised."

In an attempt to justify the actions of the government, to smooth over the appalling impression given by the migration from west to east and back of huge masses of desperate people, bourgeois students of the question invoked the theory that all the blame lay with the eastern steppelands themselves. These lands, they maintained, were barren and unusable because of their natural features. But was there anyone in Russia who did not know that this was a slander of the rich virgin steppes that had been amassing fertility for centuries?

"The soil here is good for grain, vegetables and cattle," wrote S. U. Remezov, the author of *A Sketch Book of Siberia*, about Siberia and North Kazakhstan as long ago as the eighteenth century. Ridiculing the inventions of the pseudo-scientists, Lenin wrote more than once: "There are still vacant lands ... excellent lands, which should be opened up!" In Volume 13 of his *Collected Works*, on page 253, I found an amazingly profound observation. Here he writes that these lands are unsuitable "not so much because of the *natural* properties ... but because of the *social* conditions of the agriculture ... which doom technical methods to stagnation and the population to rightless status, downtroddenness, ignorance, and helplessness. ..."

The October Revolution fundamentally changed the "social conditions" of agriculture and thus created opportunities for making use of the new lands everywhere—in Western Siberia and North Kazakhstan, in the Volga country and the North Caucasus, in the Urals and our Far East. By 1940 the country's crop area had grown by 32.4 million hectares compared with 1913. The next stage in the cultivation of the USSR's land reserves was launched in the mid-fifties, when the urgent need for grain from the virgin lands coincided with the real opportunity of fulfilling this historic mission.

The Party had for long been preparing to launch this major advance into the new lands. In the late twenties N. M. Tulaikov, a scientist of world renown, who had the vision to see that the creation of large mechanised farms would offer the prospect of taming the virgin lands, organised the first expedition to make an accurate survey of usable land in the country's eastern regions. He wrote about the success of the expedition in articles and in a memorandum to the Central Committee of the CPSU(B). In 1930, the 16th Party Congress—incidentally Tulaikov was admitted to the Party as a probationary member at this congress—debated the question of expanding grain farming in the eastern regions. The Party's position was clearly expounded in the report on "The Collective Farm Movement and the Intensified Development of Agriculture", prepared by the agricultural department of the Central Committee. Here is this interesting and far-sighted document:

"...With wheat we shall go where more valuable crops cannot grow and where the tractor can work 24 hours a day. According to the calculations of Professor Tulaikov, a new probationary member of the CPSU(B), and one of the world's greatest experts on dryland farming, there are in Kazakhstan from 50 to 55 million hectares that may be considered suitable for sowing, of which nearly 36 million lie in the northern districts adjoining Siberia and the Urals: Aktyubinsk, Kustanai, Petropavlovsk, Akmolinsk, Pavlodar and Semipalatinsk. Here wheat crops occupy only 5 per cent of the whole arable area.

"How do we intend solving this problem? It must be borne in mind that the wheat problem will have to be solved in areas of very low population density, in areas where the terrain will allow the tractor and the combine to be used with maximum efficiency. . . . It will take approximately 700,000 to one million horsepower to bring an additional 20 to 25 million hectares under wheat. This we can and should undertake!

"The organisational key to this problem is minimum use of personnel and animals, so that large reserves do not have to be kept there to safeguard against harvest failure. Besides overall mechanisation, there must be a full work load for the tractors, for every machine, every person. Here the basic assumption must be that one person should serve 200 hectares."

These proposals were adopted by the congress and supported and approved by the people. The central and local press wrote a lot at the time about the need to open up the virgin lands. The USSR People's Commissariat of Agriculture began setting up the first grain-growing state farms in Kazakhstan and Siberia and their experience helped us later, when organising the broad advance into the virgin lands. It will be readily understood, however, that in those years the country could not yet send enough machinery into the vast expanses of the steppe. Then came the war. But the idea of broad-scale opening up of the virgin and abandoned lands did not perish. Like the soil itself, it lived in expectation of its hour of destiny.

In 1974, in a speech at a conference in Alma-Ata to mark the 20th anniversary of the opening up of the virgin lands I said that the true significance of historical events and major political decisions does not usually come to the fore at once, does not appear hotfoot in their track, but only much later, when it is possible to compare the intent with the result achieved, to evaluate the actual effect of these events and decisions on this or that aspect of life. Historical distance tones down the details and brings out the salient, fundamental features. And the main thing about the virgin lands project is that in 1954 the Party set an extremely important and urgent national economic task. And this main thing was fully understood and appreciated by the Soviet people.

Let us recall the situation in the early 'fifties. The grain situation in those years gave serious cause for concern. The country's average grain yield was not more than 9 centners per hectare. In 1953 only a little over 31 million tons of grain were laid in, as against the 32 million tons that were consumed. This meant that we had to draw on the state reserves.

Cardinal, decisive and, above all, urgent measures were required to remedy this situation. In these conditions the Party, without diverting its attention from the problem of increasing the yield in the old agricultural regions, spotlighted the task of achieving a significant and rapid expansion of the crop areas. This could be done only at the expense of the virgin lands in the east.

I particularly want to stress that the expansion of crop areas was qualitative as well as quantitative. The country was not only in need of grain; it was experiencing an

acute shortage of that most valuable food
crop–wheat. And this could be provided
only by the virgin lands, where top-quality
wheat of the durum and strong varieties
could be grown. If all went well, this would
bring about a radical and, I would say, revolutionary change in the country's grain
balance.

Today, from a long distance in time, and
with the results patently obvious, everything seems incontrovertible. One even
wonders how there could have been any
opponents of the virgin lands project. But
there were. However, only the members of
the anti-Party group that was soon to be
formed could be described as real opponents, fierce opponents, determined not to
hear anything about the virgin lands. These
people should not be confused with quite
another kind, those who were mistaken, who
had sincere doubts or were overcautious.
These we tried simply to convince with facts
and figures. There was nothing malicious
about their position. Healthy doubts are
essential in any big undertaking. After all,
one has to weigh thousands of pros and
cons, consider everything down to the
smallest detail, and plan for rapid and
certain victory, and nothing but victory!

There were quite substantial grounds for all kinds of doubts. Take the purely natural factors, climatic and agricultural. Unlike many other countries, particularly the United States, where the conditions for agriculture are close to the ideal, our country is largely situated in a zone of so-called high-risk agriculture. So was it worth intensifying the effect of this factor, becoming even more dependent on nature by creating new huge-scale agricultural regions where crop farming was, in the opinion of some specialists, quite impossible? After all, it would mean sowing tens of millions of hectares of wheat in drought-ridden, heat-scorched steppes, with a precipitation of 200 or, at most, 300 millimetres a year.

This was why the gigantic project was so thoroughly discussed. In those days I was told of one episode in which K. E. Voroshilov was involved. He had returned from one of his regular trips round the agricultural regions. He came back worried, almost despondent. On learning that the question of opening up the virgin lands was being discussed and realising that this would demand huge amounts of money, manpower and machinery, he remarked sadly, "And in the Smolensk villages they're still pulling their ploughs themselves in some places. . . ."

The Party was faced with a by no means easy choice. It was only the ninth year since the war. The wounds were still bleeding. The fascists had burned and destroyed 70,000 villages, sacked 98,000 collective farms and 1,876 state farms, driven away 17 million head of cattle and 7 million horses. In the areas that had not suffered enemy occupation, the material and technical base of the machine-and-tractor stations, state and collective farms was badly crippled. The machines had been worked for years till they were past repair, the fields were in a state of neglect. And worst of all, there was a universal shortage of manpower—millions of tractor drivers, combine operators, truck drivers, mechanics, engineers and agronomists had been killed in the war.

Tremendous efforts had restored the prewar level of agricultural output but the countryside was still in need of assistance. Agriculture was not satisfying the growing requirements of the population for food, or those of industry, for raw materials.

The September 1953 Plenum of the CPSU Central Committee endorsed a wide-ranging programme designed to eliminate the defects in the guidance of agriculture. Surely, then, logic itself, the difficult position with ready cash, with material, technical and manpower resources, demanded that all forces be channelled into the traditional crop-farming areas, so as to receive a corresponding return.

But the Party's programme, though designed to boost all branches of agriculture, did not ensure and could not ensure immediate success. This was particularly true of the main objective—grain production. Increased returns in field cropping, plant growing is usually a lengthy process. So, even if it involved risk, we had to gain time by boldly channelling part of our funds and resources to the virgin lands, which promised a solid increment in the country's badly strained grain balance within a single season. The first 13 million hectares of virgin land earmarked for cultivation in 1954 could, if all went well, put an additional 800-900 million poods* of marketable grain

---

* Pood=0.01638 metric tons, roughly 16 kilogrammes.—*Tr.*

in our granaries that very autumn. And this was the course the Party took. In doing so it gained both the tactical advantage of an immediate and tangible result in the shape of grain, and the strategical advantage which lay in the fact that we were going out to the virgin lands not lightly equipped for "snatching" their riches, for skimming the cream of their fertility and going home again, but to stay there for a long time to come.

Incidentally, Kliment Voroshilov was among those who knew how to judge whether a major state undertaking was timely or premature. He came out in favour of the virgin lands and later, on visiting Kazakhstan and seeing the boundless wheatfields, he said to me joyfully:

"What a good thing we came here! The help that the Byelorussian, Smolensk and Vologda people need is ripening here on these broad expanses. And it's coming in an express ambulance. Why, we could even paint yellow crosses on the trucks with the virgin land grain, to match the colour of the wheat.... It's a grand help to us, a grand help!"

But all this came later. At the time, in 1953-1954, the debate continued. One of the most formidable objections was: How could one possibly contemplate moving such a huge armada into absolutely bare and uninhabited steppes without any rear services? No, first of all one must build settlements, schools, hospitals, roads, repair factories and shops, elevators, and only after that bring in the machines and personnel.

What answer could one give to that? Of course, it would have been good to have all these things. But those who put the question in this way did not understand the main thing—grain was needed from the virgin lands at once! We were going there to settle those lands, make them habitable and take the grain all in one operation. In establishing socialism Soviet people have often had to start with next to nothing in order to gain time. The Party openly told those it called upon to join the project: it's going to be difficult, very difficult; it will be a battle and any battle demands heroism. And hundreds of thousands of patriots consciously undertook to perform this feat.

Traditionally, the Party never takes major and fundamental decisions without consulting the people. And this was no exception.

At the end of 1953 and the beginning of 1954, the hundreds of meetings and conferences that were held in the territories and regions of the Russian Federation, Kazakhstan and other republics showed that the Communists, the broad mass of the people approved and supported the Party's idea of opening up the virgin and abandoned lands.

Of course, in the places where the battle for the virgin lands was actually to unfold there was also controversy and doubt. But there are doubts and doubts. When people realised that the Party was not planning just an easy raid into the virgin lands, but that it had worked out and prepared a grand-scale national economic programme, they supported it without hesitation. The story told by a man I have already mentioned in these notes, V. F. Makarin, first secretary of the Atbasar District Party Committee, who became a Hero of Socialist Labour on the virgin lands, is characteristic. This is what he wrote about his misgivings of those days:

"Now that many years have passed and much has been forgotten, one could brag a little and say that all of us who were in one way or another drawn into the orbit of the virgin lands were prepared, like cavalrymen with bared sabres, to charge into the attack on the silent steppe and take it by storm. But this would be contrary to the truth. To be quite honest, I must say that when we learned what was in store for the Atbasar people, I and my colleagues in the district leadership were, to put it mildly, taken aback. And this is not so hard to understand. We, who had been born, had grown up and worked in these parts, knew what the virgin land was like. We knew how grudgingly it yielded to the peasant. It was no accident that in more than a hundred years the Atbasar peasants had been able to plough only 100,000 hectares of virgin land and had sowed only a third of it, and this only in the best, most favourable years. But now within the next two years our district was to open up nearly half a million hectares, plough nearly the whole steppe and make it bear grain! That was something to think about. . . . No, we had not the slightest doubt that the country would provide us with enough machines. By that time it had a developed industry and massive economic resources. But who, may I

ask, was going to operate those machines?
The machines have not yet been invented
that can by themselves, without human
participation, plough, sow and harvest
grain, and turn it into loaves. Some people
may accuse me of exaggeration, but I am
speaking of what it was really like in those
days. We were embarking on a great and
unknown undertaking and it contained a
considerable element of risk."

My old acquaintance Vasily Filippovich
Makarin was right. There was a risk, and
the district Party Committee secretary had
every reason to ponder on how best to
perform the task set by the Party. In fact,
he was bound to. It was also right that the
district Committee frequently assembled
the activists of the Party, Soviets and
farms, and that they argued till they
were hoarse, suggesting various courses of
action.

"But our doubts," Makarin concludes,
"were soon dispelled. The Party had worked
out all the measures that we could wish for.
It was relying on the people's boundless
trust, on their high civic awareness and
enthusiasm. The machinery soon began
flowing into our district, thousands of

letters arrived from young people asking
for the addresses of collective and state
farms that needed help. Hundreds of specialists, splendid technical experts came out
to us in response to the Party's appeal. And
the unprecedented heroic task began."

5

In the old dictionaries you will find the term "virgin land", but not the term "virgin lander". It was coined in the 'fifties, just as the term "collective farmer" was coined during the years of collectivisation. The very concept of virgin land lost its purely agricultural connotation. It became a social term, implying a high sense of civic responsibility and Soviet patriotism. The virgin lander is a historic figure and represents a heroic age. And the word connotes the special character shaped by the demands of that time.

One day, when I arrived at one of Kustanai Region's state farms where only one small house was ready for the newcomers and people were still living in tents and dug-outs, I learned that the best room had been given to a young couple who had just

had a son. Everyone was celebrating the
occasion and the happy father told me:
"We've only just arrived, but you can already consider us native virgin landers."

"No," I replied, "the only native virgin
lander in this whole farm is the boy that
has been born here. You have yet to take
root. I don't think it'll happen all at once,
and it won't be easy."

I recall the talks I had long ago in Tselinograd Region and in that same Atbasar
District—first in spring, and then in autumn.
There was an entirely different ring about
them. During the first spring on the virgin
lands I heard complaints from the directors
that by no means all the newcomers intended to stay. A. V. Zaudalov, the director of
the Marinovka State Farm, told me, "On
the one hand, the people are a mixed lot,
and on the other, they're like the army—
all young folk. Here today, gone tomorrow."

"Yes, it's a problem," I agreed. "The
young are always out for adventure. In a
year or two some of them will begin to
leave. You can see for yourself, most of them
want to live only in tents. They want it
rough so that they have something to overcome. They'll build everything needed for

a start, they'll do their job, get bored and take off for other parts."

"And what shall we do?"

"Think how to keep your cadres. I see two ways of doing it. Invite some girls here. Milkmaids, seeder operators, telephonists, cooks, doctors, teachers. Isn't there plenty of work for them already here, and plenty more on the new lands tomorrow? Invite the girls, and many of the lads will stay on for good. And the second way is to invite family people, but you'll have to create normal conditions for them beforehand. That's how we'll settle this land."

What we were really talking about was planning human happiness. Everyone needs a home, love, children. Neither the state, nor society can find anybody the "chosen one", as they used to say in the old days, but they must try to see to it that there are no purely "male" regions or "female" towns. And if the demographic problems are dealt with competently, the young people will find each other and be happy. And happy they must be because without that the country cannot prosper.

It was Atbasar District that soon became the initiator of inviting girls, young women to the virgin lands. On returning to Alma-

Ata I was gratified to read in *Pravda* on July 17, 1954 a letter from young women of the Marinovka State Farm, Raisa Yemelyanova, Alexandra Zamchy, Yelena Kleshnya, Valentina Nepochatova, Polina Pashkova and Lyudmila Semyonova, appealing to girls and women across the country to come to the virgin lands. The response was tremendous. When I returned to Atbasar in autumn, at harvest-time, I met Zaudalov again. He was both glad and extremely worried.

"What's up?" I asked.

"Well, for goodness sake, Leonid Ilyich! It seems I'm not the director here any more, but the head postman.... The farm has been getting thousands of letters from girls. They're all ready for the road, they all want to come here and nowhere else! Things ought to be regulated somehow. There are plenty of other farms. Otherwise this one will be more like a fair for brides than a state farm!"

The "girl invasion" caused a good many headaches. But life on the virgin lands changed literally before our eyes. More and more rapidly it ceased to be "army" or "campaign" life and acquired normal elements of comfort. And today, no matter

where I go on the new lands I always meet
workers who were born here. Life in these
parts has put down deep and strong
roots.

Hero of Socialist Labour Zhansultan Demeyev goes out to the fields with his son,
Mirash Demeyev. This soil knows not only
the famous pioneer virgin landers, Mikhail
Dovzhik and Vladimir Dityuk, but also their
sons, the good farmers Vladimir Dovzhik
and Grigory Dityuk, who were born here.
More than once I have visited the Zhdanov
State Farm, in the North Kazakhstan Region, and met its director Mark Pavlovich
Nikolenko. When this veteran retired, the
directorship of the farm was taken over by
his son–Vladimir Markovich Nikolenko.
Amangeldy Isakov, a combine operator at
the Lenin State Farm, Karasu District, Kustanai Region, became a Hero of Socialist
Labour on the virgin lands. And his son
Vladimir is today the chief agronomist of
the Koibagar State Farm in the same
district. Ivan Grigoryevich Kosmych, combine operator of the Samara State Farm,
Tselinograd Region, has founded a real
farming family: he has nine sons who work
with him growing and harvesting the grain!
I could quote any number of such examples.

Everything went according to plan: the new lands were brought into cultivation and people took to living there.

The virgin land tent used by M. E. Dovzhik's team has for long been on display in the Museum of the Revolution in Moscow. Hundreds of steppeland towns have grown up where those tents and dug-outs once stood. Today 1,200,000 people live and work on the farms in the virgin land districts of Kazakhstan. These places have become just as settled as any of the country's other economic areas.

Photographs of the first years on the new lands revive many memories. Bare steppe, tractor columns, stakes bearing the names of the farms, tents, dug-outs, crowded trailers and mud huts with flat roofs, known as "sailor-caps". People used to huddle together in these dwellings by the dim light of lanterns and oil lamps. Everything was temporary, comfortless, rough and ready. But look at their faces—how merry, joyful they are. Every smile, every gesture conveys confidence and optimism. All of us who were working on the virgin lands in those days felt this optimism, this state of mind of people aware of their own strength. And how impressive was the steppe that we had

wakened to life! Everything was on the
move, converging on this frontline area, as
before a big offensive. Anyone who came
to the virgin lands in those days could not
help feeling involved in its interests and
aspirations.

No one denies that some people left the
virgin lands. Some were birds of passage,
self-seekers who made impossible demands
and refused to take anything into account
but their own interests. They were aptly
nicknamed not "pioneers" but "my-oneers",
and I ran into some of them during my very
first trip round North Kazakhstan. In the
early spring of 1954, at the station of Tobol
I had scarcely stepped out of the train when
a loud-voiced young man bounced up to me
out of the crowd and literally bombarded
me with questions. Where had they been
brought to? Why had they been talked into
coming here? Where was the accommodation, the good wages, the warm clothing?
Only a marmot in its hole could live in this
steppe!

I listened patiently, then said that this
was why they had been invited, to make
these places habitable. But the lad was not
to be placated. He showed his flimsy jacket
and demanded to be given a sheepskin im-

mediately. Clearly this was not the kind of person you could argue with—one always senses that kind at once—and I had to cut him short.

"Did you expect to find everything ready and waiting for you? What was the idea of coming here in that bit of a jacket and cap? The virgin lands don't need people like you!"

"Ah, it's always like that," he replied on a less strident note, "when you start demanding your legitimate rights."

"No, lad," I said, "your demands will be legitimate a month from now, perhaps two or three, and even then only in part. And they will be fully legitimate only after a year. At present there are just as many claims that can be made on you. What are you here for? We were relying on you, and now we shall have to chase around for a replacement. And you can be sure we will find one."

As far as I remember, this lad was in the group from the town of Shuya. And, of course, he was an exception to the rule. Shuya sent us some real hard workers. They named the farm in the Turgai steppes "Shuisky" after their city, and it became one of the best on the virgin lands.

There were difficulties and there is no
point in concealing the fact. Through heroic
decades our people sacrificed a lot in the
name of the future. They suffered many
grave ordeals. At various stages we were
short of everything—nails and kerosene,
shoes and the simplest kinds of cloth, a
roof over our heads, even bread. But the
Party always told the people openly: We
will overcome the difficulties and shortages
by common, persistent effort and our life
will gradually get better and better. It
did get better every year, despite the fact
that the country often had to face new
trials.

Of course, people who had to bear the
hardships of certain periods in our history
found life by no means easy, and sometimes desperately hard. In this sense Soviet
people of every generation experienced difficulties. No people on earth has endured
such trials as ours. But look at our life as
a whole. It has been on the upgrade all the
time. No matter what the obstacles, we have
always surmounted them. And our present
day is as different from the past as a space-
ship is from a peasant wagon.

But let's go back to the deficiencies that
one encountered on the new lands when they

were being opened up. They were indeed temporary. Only the egotists who did not want to lift a finger for the common cause failed to realise this. For that kind of individual the people have an apt phrase–they're only out for themselves.

But the young folk one met who had simply lost their bearings in the new surroundings were a different matter. It was enough to have a talk with them, to explain and persuade, and show a little fatherly kindness. Yes, winning with kindness was a term I often used when discussing matters with the people in charge. A young man with no experience needs some strictness but he also needs kindness. In that spring of 1954 at the station of Jaltyr, near Tselinograd, I noticed a lad with a suitcase. He obviously wanted to get on a train.

"You're not going home, are you?"

"Yes, I am."

"Rough, is it?"

"Yes. I didn't know my own nature. I never thought I'd miss home so much. It's warm there. I can see the Azov Sea from our window. The orchards are in bloom. Here it's just snowstorms and blizzards. And now these terrible winds. . . ."

I sat down beside him.

"It's always hard to begin. But just think of the young men of your age fighting at the front. They missed their homes and mothers too, they lived in dug-outs. And besides that, they had to face death in the attack. . . . Nothing big ever comes easy. It's no problem to grow an orchard in the Ukraine, but here in this steppe an orchard would be a big achievement. And yet in a year or two's time there'll be villages and orchards here as well. The main thing is to have faith in yourself. You mustn't begin life with a retreat!"

That lad, I remember, did not get on the train. I saw him later in the back of a lorry. I don't know the name of that boy, of course, now not a very young man, but I think he is among those who decided to link his future with the feather-grass steppes.

"Human existence is impossible in the wilderness of the virgin lands," a bourgeois newspaper wrote in those days. "We can rest assured that the virgin lands will remain an undigested lump in the Russian stomach."

How many other scathing prophecies of that kind were to be heard in those days! And yet within three months of the arrival of the first trainloads of volunteers

the steppe was green with boundless fields
of wheat. The republic's crop area doubled,
and in that year reached 20 million hectares.
And if, as our ill-wishers wrote, we were
"not ready" for the virgin lands, who was
it that ploughed and sowed these lands?
Who was it that gave us more than 22,000
new tractors and more than 10,000 new combines that year? Who was it that sent us
thousands of trainloads of houses, timber,
cement, merchandise, and food? No, this
was a well thought-out, properly planned
offensive. And the centuries-old fortress
named "virgin lands" fell not to a prolong-
ed siege, but to a rapid onslaught, a heroic
assault.

The question may be asked: but if these
people went out into the steppe equipped
with powerful machinery and feeling that
they had the whole country, the whole people behind them, if even then they were being sung as national heroes and from the
outset began to reap the fruits of their en-
viable renown, has not all that the term
"virgin lander" stands for been exaggerat-
ed? No, it has not. These people really did
perform a feat.

The heroic manifests itself in various
ways. A man may rush into a burning house

at the risk of his life but prove incapable of going on day after day at a monotonous job. There is the heroism of the moment. There is the heroism of grave periods in the life of the people, the war being an example. And there is the heroism of the daily round, when people consciously and voluntarily commit themselves to hardships which they know they could avoid elsewhere. I am of the opinion that the virgin land people showed themselves to be heroes. They stood up to all the difficulties of daily life in the first period and then for years laboured on patiently and steadfastly, making this far from gentle land a good place to live in.

During the celebrations of the 20th anniversary of the virgin lands I spoke in Alma-Ata about an amazing man—Ivan Ivanovich Ivanov. He was born in Leningrad. During the war he defended his native city, was gravely wounded and lost both legs. After a long period of treatment he arrived in Kazakhstan, and there he stayed. He adopted this country and the country adopted him. He developed into a fine machine operator and to his war medals were added awards for labour—two Orders of Lenin and a Hero's Gold Star.

The whole hall applauded, and so did I from the rostrum. Then other speakers took the floor and one of them told what sounded to me like my story. He too spoke of a Communist, a Leningrader, a war veteran, who had lost both legs, come to the virgin lands, become one of the best tractor drivers and a Hero of Socialist Labour. But in this story the man's name was Leonid Mikhailovich Kartauzov.... Again everyone began to clap and I wondered whether this was some coincidence. Or had I got the hero's name wrong? But no, that was impossible, I remembered him well.

In the interval I asked about Kartauzov and it turned out that there had been no mistake. Both Kartauzov and Ivanov work on the virgin lands, their fates have been similar and they are both Heroes. That is a coincidence which I would describe as symbolic. Not for nothing has the term "virgin lander" become for us a symbol of courage.

In the course of my life I have often observed that in ordinary circumstances true heroes are, as a rule, modest and not very noticeable people. They simply do their job. Such a man was Daniil Nesterenko, a tractor driver of the Dalny State Farm, Tselinograd Region. The name of the farm ("Distant") speaks for itself; it is situated in the remotest corner of the region. And this was where Nesterenko volunteered to go. The snowy winter was drawing to a close and the tractor team he worked in was in danger of being cut off from the farm centre and running out of fuel. The Zhanyspaika, an insignificant little river, might, so the local people said, burst its banks and flood the surrounding country. While it was still iced over the tractors had to be driven across. Nesterenko helped his comrades to perform this rather risky operation, and only then set out in his own tractor. But the melting ice, already half under water, gave way. . . .

When his friends pulled him out they found in the dead man's pocket a Hero of the Soviet Union's card. Until then no one in the farm had known they had such a person working with them. It transpired that Daniil Nesterenko had won his Hero's title for the forcing of the Dnieper during the war. And this made his death doubly sad. I remember the Dnieper, I remember the heroes of that crossing under deadly fire. Surely a little steppeland river was no obstacle to such a veteran! But such tragic accidents do happen.

One detail struck me as particularly moving. In Nesterenko's tent his friends found some Ukrainian cherry saplings. He must have come to Kazakhstan to stay if he had brought these young trees with him to plant in the steppe. But he was not there to see them grow.

The winter of 1954 was a severe one, with unusually heavy snow and frost. Right from the start, the virgin land put the newcomers to the test and hit out at them with its fierce, unfriendly temper. The biting winds howled incessantly and every journey across the steppes was exceptionally difficult and could be dangerous. And yet thousands of tractors, hundreds of truck convoys had to get through to the still non-existent state farms over roadless country, through the wind and snow.

What a snowstorm in the steppe is like many can imagine from their childhood reading of Pushkin's *The Captain's Daughter.* I, too, have seen how deceptive the steppe can be. At one moment the frosty sky may be blue from horizon to horizon and bright with sunshine, but half an hour will pass and you won't be able to see a thing amid a howling, whirling, whistling snowstorm. One small mistake, a mere chance, an unexpected engine failure and a man may be left all alone in the steppe with no road to follow, in bitter cold and pitch darkness.

I remember how shocked everyone was by the death of Vasily Raguzov, a correspondence-student at the Lvov Construction Institute. He had been one of the first to arrive at the Kiev State Farm and was working as a building foreman. A capable organiser and a good comrade, jolly and sociable by nature, he quickly won the respect and affection of his fellow-pioneers. On one of those clear days Raguzov was with a convoy bringing prefabricated houses from the station for the state farm's first street. Suddenly they were hit by an exceptionally fierce blizzard that went on for several days. The convoy stopped. Vasily decided to go for help on foot. He set off alone, lost his way and perished. He was a brave man with tremendous willpower. Here is a letter that was found in his pocket.

"To the person who finds this notebook! Dear Comrade, be so good as to pass on what is written here to Serafima Vasilyevna Raguzova, 15 Goncharov St, Flat 1, Lvov.

"My dear Serafima! There's no need for tears. I know it will be hard for you but what can I do now that this thing has happened to me. There's nothing but steppe all round, and no end to it. I'm just following my nose. The storm is nearly over but there's no sign of the horizon that could give me my bearings. If I don't come back, bring up our sons to be decent human beings. Ah, life! How I long to live! Lots of kisses. Yours forever, Vasily."

Realising that death was near, he wrote a postscript with numbed, frozen fingers.

"To my sons Vladimir and Alexander Raguzov. My dear children, Vovushka and Sashunka! I came out to the virgin lands so that our people would have a richer, better life. I want you to continue my work. The main thing in life is to be a human being. A big kiss for you, my dear ones. Your Dad."

This letter, so it would seem, was of a purely personal, family nature. But it became an appeal to all the living. When I was shown the pages with their blurred letters and managed to read them, I felt a tightening in the throat. I rang up the papers and suggested that, if they could obtain the wife's permission, they should publish this letter. When it was printed it evoked a response from tens of thousands all over the country. New parties of volunteers

came to the virgin lands to complete the
work begun by Vasily Raguzov and other
brave people like him. The hill near which
Vasily had died now bears his name.

The present-day map of Kazakhstan testifies to the fact that the virgin lands were
indeed opened up by the whole country. Its
geography is reflected in the names of the
state farms—"Moscow", "Leningrad",
"Minsk", "Kiev", "Dnepropetrovsk", "Ar-
mavir", "Poltava", "Tagil", "Sochi",
"Perm", "Yaroslavl", "Voronezh".... On
many of the farms one met people of other
nationalities besides the Kazakhs, the native
inhabitants of the steppe. The virgin lands
became a true school of internationalism, a
depository of the wisdom and experience,
the skills, the will to win of all peoples of
our country.

New lands are always pioneered by new
people. But here there was a special fea-
ture. We had moved a long way ahead since
the times of the first five-year plans, when
the volunteers came to Magnitka, the Turk-
sib Railway, the Dnieper Dam or Komso-
molsk-on-Amur with only saws and shovels.
The virgin lands' prime need was for tractor drivers, electricians, truck drivers, mechanics and builders, and people with these

skills were sent to us from many republics, territories and regions of the USSR. They formed the backbone of the new economic units.

People raised grain on the land and the land raised people. Metaphorically speaking, the virgin lands yielded a rich harvest of hard workers, patriots, people of skill and dedication. But coming, as they did, from all parts of the country with their own peculiarities, characters, experience and inclinations, they did not knit together automatically. And here I feel I must say a word about the methods of the Party's organisational and ideological work that we had to evolve. The Party's whole activity on the virgin lands was an epic of innovation, and an extremely successful one.

In atmosphere it most nearly resembled the political work during a big offensive operation. For me those first months entailed endless journeys and hundreds of meetings and brief encounters when people could not be interrupted for too long and I myself was short of time because I always had to push on, because I felt constantly drawn towards the "frontline". I wanted to go everywhere, to be in a dozen places at once, which was, of course, impossible, though it

all did work out somehow. The essence of
Party political work at that time was to
unite this huge mass of people and give
them a concrete programme of action and
a clear awareness of the common goal.

I remember how in my car or during long
tramps across the steppe, at night in the
tents and in the evening by the campfires I
would repeat the same thing over and over
again to the Party secretaries. The message
ran approximately as follows: bring the
Communists together more often, the first
thing is for them to get to know each other,
discuss the situation, weigh each other up.
Then they will be able to lead.

"We have nowhere to hold Party meetings," I was told.

"It's essential," I insisted.

"There's a bit too much criticism flying
around," some would object. "We haven't
got this, they haven't sent us that.... You
know what it's like at the beginning."

"Never mind," I said. "Keeping quiet
won't make things any better. When people
get together, argue and bring it all out in
the open, you'll soon find them offering a
solution themselves. And the next time, you
must report to them what's been done. People have come here from all over the country

and they're very mixed—that's the main difficulty. But there is also an advantage. There's
a real hard job to be done and it quickly
shows what a man is made of."

That first spring all my energies were
concentrated on swinging that enormous
machine into motion and there was no time
to stop and rest.

And then came the long-awaited and
nevertheless unexpected bumper grain crop
from the virgin land.

6

I shall never forget the first autumn on the virgin lands, the autumn of 1954. At a meeting at one of the state farms of Ruzayevka District, Kokchetav Region, they presented me with a sheaf of "akmolinka", virgin land wheat. My feelings as I held that sheaf in my hands were inexpressible. Memories came crowding into my mind—the first plans and concepts, the sleepless nights, the arguments, the trainloads of people, the tractor columns battling their way across the roadless blizzard-swept expanses, the first campfires in the steppe, the first furrows. And here it was before my eyes, a dream come true—the steppe yellow with wheat from horizon to horizon. . . . I remembered the handful of pioneers, the very first virgin landers, who soon after the revolution had founded the farming communes in these parts. Referring to the workers of the Obukhov and Semyannikov factories who had decided to go to Kazakhstan, Lenin wrote in a note to the People's Commissar of Agriculture: "Their initiative is excellent; support it in every way."

The first communes in the Ishim steppe had joyous names: "Ray of Revolution", "Light of Truth", "Road to the New Life". But how poorly equipped were these small settlements on the virgin lands. The Ray of Revolution Commune, for instance, had four bullocks, eleven cows, one reaper, one mower, four harrows, eight wagons, four houses and a barn. What willpower and belief in victory was needed to be able to say: "You are going to yield to us, steppe! You shall become our provider!" And now, instead of those tiny islands there was a steppe-wide ocean of wheat. The old-time plain with its waving feather-grass was becoming one of the state's greatest granaries. This was the first result of the first year's work on the virgin lands.

The wheat ocean rolled across the steppe, the wind rippled its heavy waves, the sun gilded them, and everyone was in an elevated mood. But how much energy was still needed to bring home all that grain!

Today the new lands of Kazakhstan have a massive system of large elevators and grain storage sheds. But in those days the total storage capacity did not exceed three million tons, including the primitive barns and various kinds of mud huts which the virgin landers that autumn dubbed "dog kennels". The grain had to be harvested, stored and dispatched at all costs. A particularly difficult situation developed on the roads, at the stations and at the grain-transporting junctions.

Let me describe just one episode. It happened when I flew into Atbasar with Nikolai Ivanovich Zhurin, first secretary of the Tselinograd Regional Party Committee. As soon as we landed, our hosts wanted to rush us off to the state farms, to the fields, to give us the joy, as they put it, of seeing the harvest. But these invitations were just a bit too persistent and not a word was said about the local grain-procuring depot. Naturally we decided to see it first. Someone warned, "You can't go there. The drivers will tear you to bits, honestly they will! There's a colossal jam of trucks. They have to wait two days to unload!"

"Well, that's not so terrible," I said. "We've just been at Koluton station. They're in real trouble there: grain galore and not enough trucks to carry it."

We drove up to the depot. It was a kilometre from the railway. The autumn day was bright and clear. On the outskirts of the town, amid the scorched rust-brown steppe hundreds of trucks loaded with grain were standing in a queue over a kilometre long. The depot itself was like a disturbed ant-hill. Clouds of dust rose over the grunting, snorting trucks as they tried to get through to the centre of the yard, to the great heaps of grain. From nearby came the clanging and hammering of a construction site, where a new elevator was being built. The old, rather small one, was already full to overflowing. Hundreds of people were standing about with nothing to do. About twenty women were shovelling grain into sacks, which the porters would disappear with into low mud huts where seed grain was to be stored. The trucks were being unloaded entirely by hand, and only in two or three places.

I went up to one of them and scooped up a handful of grain. It was a delight to look at: the solid heavy seed shone like gold in my hands—a marvel!

We were at once besieged by the drivers.
The uproar was unimaginable, it drowned
everything. The drivers shouted that they
were being held up for days on end, they
had to spend the night in their cabs, there
was nowhere to get a bite, to wash off the
dust. But this was nothing compared with
the fact that in the steppe the grain was already mountains high. Out there in the open
it would be ruined! I let them get it all off
their chests, then said, "This is a fine way
to welcome your guests."

I don't know whether it was the calmness
or perhaps the smile that did it, but the
drivers fell silent: after all, a man deserved
to be given a hearing.

"Don't get excited, comrades," I went on,
not yet knowing myself what to do. "We'll
think of something. I give you my word,
we'll clear this jam."

I had made a promise, but what was the
answer to the problem? We walked round
the depot, inspected the elevator that was being built and would not be ready until next
autumn, and also had a look at the "dog kennels". All the time I found myself glancing
at a large strip of wasteland between the depot and the station, the so-called "separa-
tion zone". It was cluttered with all kinds

of rubbish—rusty scrap iron, chunks of ferro-concrete, refuse. It all lay chaotically amid the withered yellow weeds, coated with dust that had been accumulating for years.

"Who does this land belong to?"

"The railway."

I asked to see the chief of that section of the line. He quickly appeared and introduced himself as Baizak Permenovich Permenov. He turned out to be a sensible businesslike man, who knew his job and was also fond of a joke, for he added, "And please don't get the name wrong. A lot of people mistake me for Balzac. But I'm not a writer, I'm a railwayman. And not French either, but pure Kazakh."

The problem we had to solve was a difficult one. I asked if one of the old grain procurers could be found.

"We won't even have to look for him," Permenov replied. "Here he is, standing right beside us—Nikanor Georgiyevich Simenkov. At present he's building the new elevator, but he used to be head of the regional procurement board. He's a professor in his line."

We went into a huddle on the edge of the wasteland. I knew the district executives well, but the head of the storage depot, Povliyanenko, was new to me. I exchanged a few words with him and learned that he was a war veteran, ex-navy. But I put my first question to the railwayman:

"How many days would it take to clear this patch of wasteland and lay a branchline to it?"

Permenov made a calculation on a notepad and said, "A day for clearing and two days for laying the line."

"You're not asking for long enough. Let's say five days.... How much grain will the district be turning in?"

Zhurin replied: "More than one district uses this depot. It's a big crop and the Yesil, Balkashino and Kurgaljino districts are all sending their grain to us. Atbasar will have to receive and dispatch three million poods. At least."

"I see...." I turned to the procurer. "Can we use this space for handling the grain?"

"On the whole, we could," he replied. "But simply clearing the ground isn't enough. That would be a breach of regulations, and sheer negligence besides."

"What has to be done?"

"Plough it up, roll it, ram it. Disinfection is absolutely necessary. If we stick to the rules, you can count ten days."

"Nikanor Georgiyevich, you've had a lot of experience. Isn't there any other way?"

"I've had to get round all kinds of corners in my time," Simenkov replied. "You can't help it. . . . The ground can be burned. Spread a lot of straw and give it a thorough scorching. That will calcinate the soil and it'll be as hard as an oven floor."

"What about disinfection?"

"The heat will do that."

"Then that's the way out of the situation!"

We were all silent for a while. We seemed to have taken everything into consideration. But then the head of the procurement depot stepped in.

"No, Leonid Ilyich, I don't agree. What difference does it make where the grain is? In the steppe it's out in the open and here with me it'll be out in the open too. The whole district couldn't make a tarpaulin to cover heaps that size. It'll all be ruined!"

"We'll make sure you get all the rolling stock you need. I take that on myself."

"And what about that?" he pointed a thumb at the sky. "Will you take that on yourself too?"

It was a stiflingly hot autumn. The sun barely seemed to move, there was not a cloud in the sky, and the forecasts were encouraging. But who could guarantee against sudden rain?

"You know," Povliyanenko said, "that it is categorically forbidden to store grain in the open. I can't take such a responsibility."

It would have been easy enough to reproach him for formalism and playing safe. But there was something about this grim-faced man that I liked. Some people would say "I'll fix it!" and then do nothing. (I shall have more to say later about one such comrade with an "I'll fix it!" for every occasion.) But Povliyanenko really would have to receive mountains of grain and he would be personally responsible for it. I could feel anxiety among the other comrades too: it's all very well for you, they seemed to say, you give your instructions and off you go. But what about us? The weather's not under our command, nor are the trains. And will we get them anyway?

"All right, let's sort this out," I said. "If we leave the grain out in the far fields, it'll be ruined for sure. They have no storehouses there and when the roads are mud-bound and the frosts come, we'll never get it out. Those millions of poods will be lost, we'll destroy all belief in the virgin lands, and peo-

ple will say we're just windbags, not managers. And they'll be right. But here you have
a road, a station, rolling stock. There are
thousands of people here who will help save
the grain in an emergency. We'll bring in
troops if necessary, students, workers—
they'll turn it over and load it, they'll help.
Can't you see the difference, Ivan Grigoriyevich? Where is it safer for the grain—in
the steppe or in town?"

"Yes, everyone will help," Povliyanenko
said. "But I'll be the one to go on trial."

It was obvious that he didn't believe my
promise of real help. I didn't want to offend
him, but I had to get at his self-esteem.

"In the old days they used to say: what
a man is at the war, so he'll be on the thresh-
ing floor. You didn't lose your grip at the
front. Why should you here? There are
emergencies even in peacetime, moments
when we have to shout: 'Stand from under!'
Besides, we could equally well ask you:
didn't you know before this that there was
going to be a bumper crop from the virgin
lands? Why didn't you prepare for it six
months ago? Why didn't you do everything
in your power? Well, all right, let's allow
that we're at fault too. We'll share the
blame, half and half. But we'll hold you re-

sponsible for this patch of ground, and strictly responsible! You've got to see to it that
every scrap of grain leaves here for the elevators, where it can be processed and
stored. We shall all answer together for
this priceless grain."

The discussion ended with mutual undertakings. Ivan Grigoriyevich, in the same
gloomy way, without any grand promises
said that he would do everything he could.
I felt he could be trusted. To be quite honest, this man's stubborn obstinacy had
brought home to me, and indeed to all of
us, the full importance of the step we were
taking. It had made us think twice, weigh
all the factors. And I, in my turn, promised
not to let this station out of my field of vision.

Some people may say that this is not the
kind of thing for a secretary of the Central Committee of such a huge republic to
be doing, that it's on too small a scale. Some
comrades thought it was hardly right for
me to go into all these details myself, even
to the point of peering into the cooking pots
of the field work-teams. Didn't this reduce
the responsibility of the lower-grade officials? My reply to this is that no amount
of paperwork, no telephone calls are a sub-

stitute for meeting people and knowing life. Unfortunately I have often seen for myself that all kinds of reports, while travelling up through the departments, tend to get distorted. And always in one direction—towards toning down the awkward facts.

"Office" leadership is not enough. One must be constantly in touch with the people, go out and see with one's own eyes both the successes and the difficulties and, if necessary, effectively intervene. After an argument with the people at such a steppeland station, after sitting round the common pot with a team of tractor drivers you come to understand a lot and learn a lot. It is always a good thing to learn something new, and when such major operations as the opening up of the virgin lands are only just getting under way it is absolutely essential.

What is more, such occurrences as the one I have just described do not remain mere episodes. Not infrequently they result in major decisions. On returning to Alma-Ata I put the grain-procurement issue before the Central Committee Bureau and a decision was taken on the matter. I got in touch with N. A. Gundobin, Deputy Minister for Railways of the USSR, and told him

how urgent the problem was. In those days
he spent nearly all his time on the virgin
lands, virtually directing the main control
centre in Tselinograd. Day and night he kept
a check on the movement of freight and
turn-round of traffic and was quick enough
in responding to our requests. So the rip-
ples from that "minor" episode spread out
in circles, as it were, right across the virgin
lands.

But let me return to the episode in Atbasar. The heat that year was utterly exhaust-
ing. After the talk at the procurement depot someone suggested going down to the
river for a dip. But even there, of course,
the talk was still about business.

I said to the leaders of the district, "Despite the great difficulties you face, your district can come out well to the fore in grain
delivery. You can do it."

I did keep a close check on how things
were going at the Atbasar depot. I had to
ask the republic's Minister for Procurement
to go there urgently to render practical assistance. I telephoned frequently to ask how
much grain they had received, how much
had been dispatched and what help was
needed. All the precious grain was safely
gathered in and later, when the Atbasar

people had fulfilled their undertakings (they did become initiators of a movement for above-plan delivery), and when *Pravda* published a big article about their initiative (a good, useful initiative), I must confess that I felt a deep personal involvement in the success of the machine operators, district Party Committee people, procurers, and railwaymen. And it meant a lot to me.

In 1954, for the first time in its history Kazakhstan poured 250 million poods (over 4 million tons) of grain into our country's granaries—150 million more than in the best years before that. All of us, virgin landers, experienced the true happiness of that victory.

7

After the autumn of 1954 the advance into the virgin lands developed on an even greater scale. In addition to the 90 new state farms about 250 more had to be set up. The increase in the number of farms meant an equivalent increase in our commitments.

However, by this time the republic's Party organisation had gained experience in handling the day-to-day affairs of the virgin lands and a fairly clear-cut long-term programme of action was emerging. Many features of Kazakhstan's present-day agriculture, its structure and basic trends were determined and began to take visible shape at that time, nearly a quarter of a century ago.

What particularly worried us in those days, what questions were given priority, how the campaign for achieving our goals proceeded is partly described in my book *Questions of*

CPSU Agrarian Policy and the Opening Up of the Virgin Lands of Kazakhstan. To avoid repetition I will give only the main lines, the programme targets of those years:

by opening up the virgin and abandoned lands, and also by raising the yield on the old arable, to make grain the main branch of Kazakhstan's agriculture, to increase the production of grain there compared with the previous period not less than tenfold and thus turn the republic into a new major grain-producing area;

to evolve and gradually introduce on the virgin lands the scientific system of crop farming best suited for the extremely difficult climatic conditions and preserving and multiplying the natural fertility of the soil;

in setting up the country's largest grain-growing state farms to build for each of them everything they need—both well-equipped production premises and comfortable urban-type housing with all the normal social and cultural services and public utilities. To completely reorganise, expand and remodel on the pattern of the new farms all the old state and collective farms of the republic;

in the shortest possible time to link up the virgin land regions by means of a network of railways, highways and also inter-farm roads, to install power transmission lines, telegraph, telephone and radio communications, to build at key points large-capacity elevators, factories for producing and repairing agricultural machinery, and dozens of other enterprises, and thus turn North Kazakhstan into a highly developed economic area, functioning as one economic organism;

on the basis of increased grain production and by using its waste materials, and by means of a sharp expansion of the area under fodder crops, particularly maize, and also by raising the yields of the grass sown and improving the hayfields, to radically strengthen the fodder base and ensure a rapid growth of livestock breeding. In the long term to at least double all types of animal products;

in the south of the republic, by means of soil improvement to intensively develop the cultivation of rice, cotton, beets, vegetables, fruit and grapes.

This programme was not an easy one. It also had to be carried out not bit by bit, but all at once. And, of course, one had to reckon with all the current difficulties and those that we were still to encounter. So it was very important to inspire everyone with whom the work brought us into contact by our faith and energy.

Take animal breeding. Quite a lot of comrades let the campaign for grain eclipse everything else and neglected other important branches of agriculture.

We resolutely set about reorganising animal breeding, for example. There were times when I was reproached for repeating some things too often. It's clear enough already, people would say, why keep on talking about the same thing? It was clear all right, but progress was slow and sometimes things did not move at all. It took a great deal of effort, for example, to develop maize, a crop that was virtually new to Kazakhstan. We intended ultimately to grow it for its grain as well, but most of the sowings were for silage. This roused a kind of tacit resistance among the local comrades. How could anyone want to raise "grass" on good ploughland? Again and again one had to argue, urge, show in practice how to sow maize, cultivate it, harvest it and silo it.

I knew the value of this crop from my experience in the Ukraine and Moldavia, but since I was no agronomist I decided to get expert opinion. I wrote a letter to M. E. Ozerny, the "maize magician", who was a friend of mine and lived in the village of Mishurin Rog, Dnepropetrovsk Region. Soon an answer arrived with some very valuable advice. At my request he also sent me varieties of seed suitable for the drylands of Kazakhstan. Things got moving but on more than one occasion we had to put the matter before the Central Committee Bureau and hold seminars on maize.

The trial sowings of the first spring had done well and in 1955 we put 700,000 hectares under this crop. Animal breeding also began to make headway, though not very quickly. It was perseverance that helped us in this, as in other matters. At a meeting of the republic's activists in March 1955, I said:

"There are some questions that one has to return to over and over again. What does this indicate? I think, on the one hand, the essential importance of the assignment, and on the other, the great difficulty of accomplishing it. Our persistence in raising these problems is yet another proof of the seriousness of our intentions. To push through our ideas we shall go on hammering away at the same spot without wavering or hesitation.

The time is bound to come when these problems will be taken off the agenda. And then—of this we are also well aware—new questions, new tasks of even greater range and scope will arise."

Some comrades could not grasp this. With the first harvest from the virgin lands it looked to them as if the final goal had been achieved. They sensed the possibility of a breather, started reshuffling their cadres and recommending some for promotion. I don't mean that the comrades in question hadn't deserved it. On the contrary I remember and deeply respect the first virgin land directors of state farms. They shouldered a massive burden and many of them later developed into high-powered managers. But at that moment it was too early to take people away from their posts.

One day I was approached by one of them, Fyodor Trofimovich Morgun. He came to me with a complaint that could hardly be described as ordinary. He had been offered a higher position, but he didn't want it and was doing all he could to get out of it. There is no need for me to describe this man in detail because he later described everything himself in a book *Thoughts on the Virgin Lands*. His state farm was also one of the best and was often cited as an example to others, so now the director had been recommended for the post of chairman of the district Executive Committee. What seemed to be an honour had upset him enormously. He had only just got the farm going, made friends with the people, worked out a plan for turning the farm into a veritable factory for producing cheap grain, and now he would have to abandon it all. I had to intervene personally, and this is what was said on the subject at a big conference.

"We cannot agree with the decision of the bureau of the Kokchetav Regional Party Committee on the transfer of Comrade Morgun, director of the Tolbukhin State Farm, to other work, even though it carries promotion. There should be no hasty transferring of personnel. They must be helped to build up the state farms, master the system of cropping with an eye to the local soil and climatic conditions, allowed to complete the work they have begun, and only then be moved up to higher posts, if this should prove necessary."

Another example. Yevdokia Andreyevna Zaichukova was nearly fifty when she came to the virgin lands. But she had kept her youthful zest, willpower and strength of character and above all she had the ardent heart of a Communist and patriot. She was moved to come to us by a profoundly conscious desire to do everything that could and should be done for the country, and it was this that gave her the energy to set up the Dvurechny State Farm in the steppes. Soon she, too, was given promotion. But after working for a while at her new post, she wrote the following application:

"I firmly request the members of the District Party Committee to release me from the post of First Secretary of the District Committee. I request this because I believe that the remaining years of my life could be spent with greater benefit to the Party and everyone on actual managerial work. I request to be sent to a backward state farm and promise that together with the Communists and all the workers there I will make it one of the foremost farms of Tselinograd Region."

And she kept her word: under her directorship the Izhevsk State Farm did very well indeed. Yevdokia Andreyevna gave seventeen years of her life to the new land that she had grown to love. And when she was dying, she asked the friends who came to see her in hospital only one thing:

"Don't put up any fences round my grave. Don't separate me from the steppe."

Such people are our greatest asset, the pride of the Party and the nation. And we treated them with special consideration. Without the knowledge of the Central Committee of the Communist Party of Kazakhstan no one had the right to move the directors and managerial staff of the state farms, let alone dismiss them. As far as I remember we replaced not more than ten directors, and these were people for whom the burden of the virgin lands proved too heavy. The same policy applied to other cadres. We actively supported the best, were patient and considerate with the promising and firmly got rid of people who obviously lacked ability or were slack.

The bumper harvest focussed general attention on the virgin lands, victory notes were sounded in the press, it became customary to praise and congratulate us, but we knew that we could not afford to relax. It was too early to rest on our laurels. Kazakhstan's Party organisation was aware that we should have to push ahead with the construction of elevators and storage facilities and get people out of the tents and dug-outs as soon as possible. This was becoming an ever more complex and urgent problem.

Literally everything had to be built from scratch. But what with? If there had been forests all round, the question would not have arisen. Admittedly, the virgin lands were receiving prefabricated houses and building materials, but not enough to go round. Our plans ran ahead of our potential and, obviously, maximum use had to be made of the local resources. But by no means everyone was being as efficient and resourceful as he could be.

Sometimes I would arrive at a district centre and ask how the construction work was going. Badly, they would say. Why? No bricks. But then we would walk down the street with the district Party Committee secretary and see solid buildings with dates on them—1904, 1912. . . . And yet I knew for a fact that there were no brickyards in this district and never had been.

"Who put up these buildings?"

"The *zemstvo*."

"Where did they get the bricks?"

"Down there in the ravine. They built a scove kiln and baked them. That's what this school is built of too."

"So the *zemstvo* could organise everything and you, the district Party Committee and the district Executive Committee can't? What kind of leaders are we? There's plenty of clay all round, make some scove kilns and in some places set up brickyards. They'll serve you for another hundred years."

"A brickyard? That's too big an undertaking for us."

It makes you angry to see people so passive!

In Barvikha, near Moscow, I happened to notice a splendid castle built of brick. It was a holiday camp for Young Pioneers. I inquired about the building and was told that it used to be part of the estate of some baroness or other. How had the castle been built? Quite simply. The rich lady had ordered a brickyard to be set up, built herself this country residence and all its outbuildings with the bricks, then sold the brickyard and completely recovered all the costs of the construction. Of course, she did not devise the whole scheme herself, she had a sensible manager. That's how it was done. But even today we have whole production teams, experienced leaders, engineers, builders who set out on grandiose undertakings but cannot build an ordinary brickyard. Instead they rely on the state and apply to the State Planning Committee.

I recall how on the virgin lands we had to borrow from some of the old stud farms the solid stable buildings constructed out of those same scove bricks. We needed them for the repair shops of machine-and-tractor stations. When I told people about this, when I managed to get through to them and make them feel ashamed, I would soon find sensible managers arranging their own brick production. Afterwards they would thank me for it and wonder why they hadn't thought of it before.

One of the local building materials was rushes. On learning that a few enterprising people had already built themselves solid houses out of compressed rush slabs, I drove out to have a look and was quite satisfied with this form of housing. It would serve well enough for the first few years. This meant that we should have to gather rushes on a big scale and get the slabs into production. I consulted a map of the republic that showed the places where rushes grew and decided to see them in their natural state. I flew along the valley of the River Ili as far as Lake Balkhash. From an altitude of 100 metres it looked like a solid jungle of rushes!

Soon we organised the procurement of rushes wherever they grew in any abundance—along the banks of rivers, around many steppeland lakes. Factories quickly manufactured simple, convenient and highly productive machines that crushed and pressed them into solid slabs. These slabs were good for assembling buildings of any shape. When plastered and whitewashed, they made splendid warm houses. After testing the process, we held a republic-wide seminar on rush-slab construction at a collective farm near Alma-Ata.

The Kazakhstan Party Central Committee attached high priority to construction problems. The files still contain our memorandum to the CPSU Central Committee on what resources the republic had at its disposal when it set out to develop the virgin lands. Our forces were scattered; more than thirty low-capacity construction organisations were subordinated to various ministries and departments. All told, they had 59 concrete mixers, 6 tower cranes, 58 carriers, 5 motor hoists, and only 5,700 workers. To fulfil the new plans we needed at least ten times that number of people!

Construction materials, particularly bricks, were, of course, a big problem. I appealed to the leaders of a number of our republics and I must say that they were most helpful. Bricks started arriving from Armenia, Georgia, Estonia and many other places. In short, we dealt with the problems as they arose and dealt with them successfully.

The Kazakhstan writers' congress in the autumn of 1954 was a major event in the cultural life of the republic.

It was not the first time I had been involved in matters connected with a national culture. Back in Moldavia I had realised that if you go to live in another republic you should get to know the customs and traditions of its people, their history and art. As soon as I arrived in Alma-Ata I laid in a stock of books, started meeting Kazakh writers and artists and going to the theatre as often as possible. I had long had a liking for poetry and I read much of the verse of the Kazakh poets, particularly Abai, whose lyricism, folk wisdom an deep knowledge of life appealed to me. Abai taught the Kazakh people not to isolate themselves, not to stand still, but to enrich their culture with the achievements of the Russian and other peoples. This message is still relevant. Any national culture that becomes wrapped up in itself inevitably puts itself at a disadvantage and loses its universal human features. Unfortunately this is not always appreciated.

Socialism has long since proved that the more intensive the growth of each national republic, the more apparent the process of internationalisation. Kazakhstan is perhaps the most vivid example of this. The virgin lands made it without exaggeration a "planet of one hundred tongues". And Kazakh culture forged ahead, absorbing all that was best in the other national cultures. Is this bad or good? We Communists reply: it's good, very good! This vital question of national traditions and originality should never be oversimplified, reduced merely to ethnography, to everyday customs and traditions: in Russia, to *izbas*, round-dances and *kokoshnik* head-dresses, and in Kazakhstan, to *yurtas* and droves of horses.

We in the Central Committee tried to give constant help to the artists and writers. Despite all the difficulties of the virgin lands campaign, it was this period that saw the

birth of the Kazakh State Song and Dance
Ensemble, the resumed publication of the
newspaper *Kazakh adebieti,* and large-scale
preparations for the ten-day festival of Kazakh literature and art in Moscow. This did
not come about without debate. Some people wanted to concentrate entirely on the
oral art of the *akyns* (bards). But deep-go-
ing qualitative changes were taking place
in the literature of the republic. They
stemmed from the progress of socialist construction and the growth of the Kazakh intel-
ligentsia. Gifted young people who knew
and loved not only the old traditions and
songs, but were well versed in Soviet and
world literature had come upon the scene.
These were people with free untrammelled
minds and they had to be supported. But
the main thing was to improve the atmosphere in the artistic unions, among the in-
tellectuals. They had to be rallied, their
forces had to be united to cope with the
tremendous tasks facing the republic.

Incidentally I would note that champions
of national exclusiveness masquerading as
defenders of "the purity of the national tra-
dition", usually act deviously and rarely
come out into the open. On the contrary,
they try to appear "holier than the pope"

by cleverly exploiting any mistakes made
by their opponents. I remember all the hue
and cry over the role of a certain Kenesary.
At first he was declared to have been a pro-
gressive figure favouring the union of Kazakhstan with Russia. Later, documents were
found indicating that he was a reactionary
and did not approve of the union. . . . I have
no desire to dig up past history, and besides
I don't regard myself as a specialist in this
sphere. What worried me was something
else. The battles that certain demagogues
provoked had made such outstanding people as the writer Mukhtar Auezov and Aca-
demician Kanysh Satpayev leave the republic.

We helped them to return to Alma-Ata.
That splendid scientist Kanysh Imantayevich
Satpayev has tremendous services to his credit in the development of Kazakhstan's productive forces. Mukhtar Omarkhanovich
Auezov is an acknowledged classic of Kazakh
literature. It is with much gratitude that I
recall these people, with whom I often met,
closely co-operated, and with whom I simply
enjoyed a very human friendship. In our talks
we often spoke of the fact that all extremes
are harmful. The oral art beloved of the people should not be forgotten either. "Lenin-

graders, my children!"–the whole country remembers those inspired lines of Jambul's. Let the art of the *akyns* live and develop in the general stream of national Kazakh and multi-national Soviet literature.

And I had yet another thought in my mind: how to focus the attention of the writers and artists on the virgin lands theme? Just look at the things that are taking place before our very eyes, I said at a meeting with writers at the Central Committee. Huge masses of people are on the move, multi-national collectives are being formed, new families are being born, characters are maturing, the heroes of our time are being tested and toughened. In Kazakhstan bread was always a delicacy, something precious. Even the mullahs used to say in the old days, "The Koran is a sacred book but one can tread on the Koran if it is necessary to reach a crumb of bread." And now this region is going to have an abundance of bread. The whole structure of life is changing, people are acquiring a new psychology. Should not the greatness, the dramatic appeal of what is happening stir the inspiration of the true artist? No one will understand us now or in the future if this epic is not vividly recorded for history.

In this situation it was important that the congress of writers of the republic should become a festival of Soviet literature as a whole. We invited Mikhail Sholokhov, Leonid Leonov, Kamil Yashen, Mirzo Tursunzadeh, Maxim Tank and other famous writers to attend. After this composers, actors and artists became frequent guests of the virgin lands, articles and stories about the battle for grain were published, motion pictures appeared, plays were produced and new songs were sung. They undoubtedly played a positive role.

It was my dream that one day the epic of the virgin lands would be reflected in works of art as profoundly and powerfully as the civil war is reflected in *And Quiet Flows the Don*, and collectivisation in *Virgin Soil Upturned*. For the writer and artist there is surely no more inspiring task than to portray the feats of the people, and this should include those performed on the virgin lands.

The year 1955 was called the "year of desperation" on the new lands. My own assessment would not be so extreme, although things were very tough. All summer, from May onwards not a single drop of rain fell. We waited in vain for the rains that come regularly in June. This meant that we had to be prepared for the worst.

Anyone who has not been in the steppes at such a time just cannot understand the feelings of the grain farmer. It is a strange sensation: in spring the steppe would sometimes be turned into a sea by floodwaters and people would have to reach their work-teams by boat. But as soon as those freshets ceased, the water disappeared. From early morning the scorching sun would begin its work of destruction. It would drift slowly across the whitish faded sky, pouring down its intolerable sultry heat until evening, when the purple-red orb would sink in a turbid haze below the horizon. And the next day, almost without respite it would rise again and go on burning the life out of everything. And this went on week after week, month after month.

Meanwhile, we had doubled the crop areas in comparison with the previous year. Nearly ten million hectares of grain had been planted on the newly cultivated lands. One and a half million hectares over and above the plan had been sown in spring. And the sowing had been carried out faster, more concertedly, better than in the previous season. In one year the republic had taken a huge step forward in crop farming. People could already see the results of their labours and continued to work with a will, not yet knowing the disaster that awaited them.

We knew, of course, that heat and drought were nothing out of the ordinary in this region. But we did not yet know the implacable perversity of the steppeland calendar, which once in ten years brings particularly cruel and destructive droughts upon the land. We foresaw, even before launching our offensive, that a battle with the elements was inevitable. When the economics of opening up the virgin lands were worked out, the experts estimated that even if there were two years of severe drought in every five we should still receive an average of 500 million poods (8 million tons) of grain per year. There was no reason to doubt these estimates. We knew what we were getting into, but it is one thing to know and quite another to see the precious harvest that has taken such effort to grow perish before your eyes.

How people crave for rain at such a time! The nervous tension builds up beyond endurance. The merest rustle against a windowpane can bring people rushing out of their homes at night. "Rain!" But no, it is not raindrops pattering on the windows and roof, but dust driven by the dry wind.

In the steppe it is difficult to breathe. The air sears the lungs like the breath of a furnace. As at times of intense cold, the birds do not fly. Plants dry up, lose their leaves and wither into dust. The ground breaks into deep cracks, big enough to swallow a crowbar. The huge masses of wheat turn grey, then white and rustle the empty ears where the grain never had time to ripen.

And to crown everything, come the hot storms, lifting clouds of dust, tearing down telegraph lines and ripping off roofs.

One can understand the pain a farmer feels when he sees how relentlessly everything is being destroyed, all the fruit of his year's work, all his efforts and hopes. And one needs a sturdy spirit and strong nerves to stand this test. Even the knowledge that next season the steppes should redeem all that has been lost does not help very much; one always wants the harvest today, now.

I have no wish to oversimplify the situation, to make things appear better than they were. In those months we at the Central Committee began to receive letters from people asking what was to be done, how to carry on.

The Central Committee Bureau of the Kazakhstan Communist Party decided to hold general meetings in all the virgin land farm production teams and honestly describe the state of affairs, put some heart into people, direct their attention to the tasks that would take priority under those conditions, and explain that in crop farming one year differs from another, and that the time would come when our virgin lands would have it good too. At the same time I warned those who went out to the districts not to act like carefree optimists. Such were the main objectives of Party work among the masses at that moment.

I must say that after the frank and open discussions that were held at every state farm the virgin landers got down to work with renewed zest. Despite the blazing sun we went on preparing for the harvest and were busy laying in stocks of animal feed right up to late autumn. We pushed ahead with construction even more widely and actively, particularly in the state farms. Food and industrial goods were coming into the virgin lands in large enough quantities to guarantee uninterrupted supplies for the whole winter.

We found support and help at the CPSU Central Committee.

My warmest appreciation is due to the members of the Political Bureau and secretaries of the CPSU Central Committee, who did so much in those years to bring the virgin lands quickly and successfully under cultivation. I often met and consulted with them and always received precise, specific answers to my questions, firm Party backing and kindly moral support.

And despite the difficulties we continued our work with confidence in 1955. What was the basis of this confidence? Certainly, we were all bitterly disappointed that the tremendous effort we had put into the soil had not produced the desired results. A number of farms, however, had reaped a decent harvest. The Zhdanov State Farm, Kokchetav Region, set up in 1954, had brought home 7.9 centners per hectare from an area of 22,500 hectares and the Roslavl State Farm, Alma-Ata Region, 9.1 centners from each of its 20,000 hectares. And such farms were not so few in number. Whole districts and even regions, such as the North Kazakhstan and the Kokchetav, gathered harvests that were not at all bad for those days. We should have to make a thorough inquiry into what had helped some to bring in their grain and what had left others with nothing but scorched fields. I must add that despite the low average yield it was from the virgin lands that the republic received 80 per cent of its total grain harvest that year. Kazakhstan again laid in considerably more coarse feed than before they were opened up, and supplied 85,000 tons more milk and 122,000 tons more meat. Nearly one and a half million tons of silage, mainly maize, were stored.

These were, of course, modest successes, but they showed that the virgin lands were already playing and would continue to play an ever increasing role in boosting output of grain and other farm produce. So keep working! That was our watchword.

But a harvest failure is a harvest failure and it made many problems much more difficult to solve.

At the end of 1955 I was in Moscow at an All-Union Meeting of Party and Government Functionaries. One feels uncomfortable, of course, at such gatherings, when people go on asking you endless questions or, on the contrary, express their sympathy by deliberately talking about something else. And when I declared from the conference platform that Kazakhstan would supply the state the following year with 600 million poods of grain, an incredulous murmur broke out all over the hall.

How times have changed! If we tried nowadays to set a target of 500 to 600 million poods a year for the virgin lands, which then seemed a great boon, it would be regarded as a serious defeat. Nowadays we receive on average about a billion poods (16 million tons) of Kazakhstan grain per year!

In Japan, as I. A. Goncharov relates in *The Frigate Pallada*, the governors of provinces in the old days used to answer with their heads for everything that happened there–typhoons, cloudbursts and earthquakes. Our heads did not seem to be in danger, but after the unfortunate course of events in 1955, one had an oppressive sense of being guilty of something for which one was not really to blame. I have not forgotten that feeling. And today I sometimes call up districts that have suffered natural disasters simply to offer a word of encouragement to the people in charge. On one occasion I was invited to Ulyanovsk Region: "Leonid Ilyich, come and see us, we've got a wonderful crop of grain!" And soon after that, the dry winds began to blow and everything was burnt up. Understandably, the first secretary of the regional Party Committee was embarrassed, upset and worried. I discussed things with him in the usual calm way. We had to agree upon what measures should be taken and how to help the comrades.

But during that year of disaster we, who all along were confident of success, sometimes had difficulty in proving that we were right. When at one of the big conferences I declared in the presence of N. S. Khrushchov that the virgin lands would yet show their true worth, he interrupted me rather sharply, "We can't make pies out of your promises!"

But I had every reason to answer him firmly, "All the same we believe that soon, very soon there will be a bumper grain crop on the virgin lands!"

We took great pains to prepare for the new spring. There was only one salvation, one hope, one remedy—work. In 1956, 27 million hectares of virgin land were to be sown, and 22 million of them to grain crops. And once again I wanted to see everything, meet everyone, get everything done in time....

In order to increase the production of grain, meat, and vegetables we now assign huge material and financial resources that were quite beyond our dreams in those years. We are installing the latest machinery, re-equipping agriculture, consistently introducing specialisation and concentration of production, and undertaking such integrated programmes as the transformation of the ancient Russian non-black-earth lands. This area is our front line today.

But there is something else one has to remember: in the national economy there is no "rear line". One still encounters some comrades who are prepared to spend millions and billions, but lose sight of the so-called trifles. And yet one of the key tasks

is to make careful and rational use of everything that we have at our disposal, that is
produced in the country. Extravagance is im-
permissible; the broader the scope of the
economy the more painful the effects of
such mismanagement.

This was brought home to me while I
was still on the virgin lands. So I do not
want to lose sight of those "trifles", upon
which a great deal in the life of the people
depends. For instance, when I was on a big
trip round North Kazakhstan, I arrived at
the Izobilny State Farm, Tselinograd Region.
It was situated in the far-out steppes, on
the River Selety, in a picturesque but at that
time very wild spot. I had been there before,
at the very beginning, and seen the first
nine tents. This time I found a whole settlement. There were apartment houses, a cafeteria, a shop, a bath-house, a bakery, work-
shops, a general office and a garage. In addition, and this was particularly important,
people had built themselves nearly eighty
private cottages. This meant that they really
had settled in for good.

I got into conversation with them and began asking what they needed and how
things were going. And this is what I
heard.

"We're short of barrels. There's nothing to salt the cucumbers in."

"We want a pig, but where can we buy one?"

"It'd be a good thing to have a calf...."

These were no idle questions. A great deal of everything had been pumped into the virgin lands. Yet here we were with a shortage of barrels. And animals were needed too. And not only as an addition to the larder. In our first year I had seen newcomers arriving, a suitcase in one hand, and a basket with a pup or a cat in the other. A lad from Zaporozhye turned up at the Yaroslavl State Farm with a live rooster in a cage. "The best alarm-clock for the steppe," he told me. A joke, of course, but on that bare earth the rooster was a joy to everyone. The lads even managed to tame marmots and some of the steppeland birds.

One could regard all this as mere whimsy. But life has taught me to understand such things and treat them with respect. In my childhood I myself loved to watch a flight of pigeons on the wing. Of course, the main thing on the virgin lands for us was the millions of hectares and billions of poods, but people had to be helped to start up their personal vegetable gardens, to raise animals and poultry. Without that the millions and billions would not have been achieved. The countryman with no livestock and plot of land in his keeping is like a tree without roots. In those years it was important for us to show from the first that we intended to make the steppe really habitable, and forever.

While pondering on this subject, I looked across the fields and suddenly noticed yet another newcomer: a lonely rook was strutting across the black ploughland like a fault-finding agronomist. And the rook, as we all know, is a field bird. Once it had flown all the way here, it must have come to stay.

I remembered the talk at Izobilny Farm and later turned up some old documents. Back in 1934 a CPSU(B) Central Committee memorandum had been sent to the Kazakhstan Territory Party Committee. It had posed very broadly and firmly the question of developing horticulture both in rural areas and in the industrial districts. Thorough to the last detail, the memorandum proposed that this sphere should be given the most active and comprehensive assistance by Party and government bodies and also the leaders of collective and state farms and cooperatives. And horticulture soon developed and acquired a reliable material base. But years passed and suddenly it started to decline, shrinking to almost half its former size. And yet the republic had been receiving two and a half times as much potatoes, for instance, from the personal vegetable patches, as from the collective and state farms.

When one criticised certain directors for feeding their people on noodles and skilly the reply was always: we're short of supplies, give us supplies! There is no denying that some products should be centrally allocated to the rural areas, too, but what allocations could they require for potatoes, cabbage, cucumbers and water melons? All that can easily be grown on any farm. The same applies to eggs and milk. From time immemorial the peasant has kept chickens and sold eggs in town. Why should he now receive every egg on a warrant from Moscow?

What I am writing about is still highly relevant today. There are still a good many executives who do nothing but rely on the almighty allocations without giving a second thought to where the state is to find them. In our country we must use every opportunity, every scrap of land to increase output of farm products, to have "a bit extra" for our common table. Sometimes from a train window one sees patches of cluttered wasteground that could very well be used for cultivation, sowing grass, keeping animals. All this would make for better supplies out of local resources, instead of having to bring, say, tomatoes and cucumbers all the way from the south, and eggs, cottage cheese, and milk from places hundreds of kilometres away.

These things must be kept in mind by Party, government and economic bodies, and by the leaders of industry. It is their duty to develop solid agricultural bases around the large and small towns, to build up the specialised complexes and the subsidiary units, so as to ensure that there are plenty of potatoes, meat, milk, greens and fruit in the shops. There are such opportunities in Sverdlovsk, in Tyumen, in Irkutsk, and in any other city of the USSR. This was something I again had to point out to the local leaders during a trip round the Urals, Siberia and the Far East in the spring of 1978.

But in Kazakhstan, way back in 1955, a decision was taken to develop kitchen gardening on a broad scale, to give everyone who wanted it a plot of land, make imple-

ments available and give every possible assistance. The same policy was adopted with
poultry and the sale of animals for personal use. It was no less important to organise
subsidiary units in all the state farms. Here
a strange situation had arisen. By the time
the virgin lands project was launched the
number of such units had dwindled almost
to a quarter. In the midst of their global
plans and grandiose projects some people
had abandoned what seemed to them of sec-
ondary importance.

These "trifles"—and figures will be of some
use here—presented the following picture:
the number of cows in subsidiary holdings
had diminished by 11,000, sheep by 280,000;
3,700 hectares of gourd crops, 5,000 hectares of vegetables and 11,000 hectares of potatoes had disappeared no one knew where.
The country was still living under difficult
conditions and yet here we were being de-
prived of a huge amount of produce. Urgent
measures had to be taken. Funds and land
were allocated for subsidiary units, **dairy**
animals were brought in, hot-houses and
poultry sheds were built, soft-fruit planta-
tions laid out; their production was written
into the plans of the state farms and the directors were held strictly responsible for

fulfilment. All this was important both for
the better supplying of the virgin landers
and to give people the psychological lift of
seeing that life in the steppe was getting
better.

Recalling all this and reading the documents of those years, I noticed how often
I mentioned Kurgaljino District. I was very
upset in those days over its affairs, and particularly by what I saw during one of my
visits to the Stepnyak State Farm. I first visited this farm in the summer of 1954 and
was confronted with a sad picture. In such
places you immediately feel that something
is wrong. People attach themselves to any
newcomer and follow him about in com-
plaining crowds. I, too, was immediately
buttonholed by a woman, who poured out
her story.

"Comrade representative, I don't know
who you are but take an interest, help us.
We haven't any electricity, any fuel, any
kerosene even. There's nothing to cook with.
And there's nothing to cook either. . . ."

I went into the local shop with her. There
was not even any salt. Another woman, with
a child, addressed me no less anxiously.

"Comrade Brezhnev, there's no milk, no
semolina. Tell us what we're supposed to

feed the children on. You must have children yourself. You're a father, so help us."

I asked to see the representative of the
workers' co-operative. Without batting an
eyelid he declared that semolina had been
out of stock for only one day. But his shifty
eyes told me he was lying. I promised the
women I would investigate the shortage of
groceries, but what surprised me even more
was the lack of milk. By then we had given
many state farms, including the Stepnyak,
animals for their workers who wanted to
keep them on a subsidiary basis. We had
asked for a report on how many cows, pigs,
horses, and poultry had been allotted and
to whom, and had let the matter rest there.
But while I was walking round the farm,
the crowd steered me into the cafeteria and
we sat down to talk things over.

"How many cows have you got in your
subsidiary farm?"

"About fifty."

"Then you ought to have enough milk."

"Some hopes! They're sixty versts away
from here. They're out there for pastur-
ing."

By this time they had found the director,
Kovalenko. He hurried in and started com-
plaining at once.

"It's terrible, Leonid Ilyich! I can't persuade any of the women to become milkmaids. None of them want to milk the cows."

"Are they not being milked while they're at pasture?"

"That's how it works out."

"Aren't you worried about the children going without milk and the harm being done to the cows?"

"Not worried? I'm scared. I'm expecting to face trial. But never mind, I'll fix it.... I've already sent a letter to the Ukraine. I'm inviting some girls to come and help us out."

It was clear what he stood for and I turned to the women.

"Why don't you want to help? You see what the situation is."

"What can we do with the children?" they burst out. "We've all got families, children."

"Suppose we distribute the cows among you for a while, then will you look after them, milk them?"

"Of course, we will! We'll milk them and drive them out into the steppe. And our husbands can milk them too."

"Well, Comrade Kovalenko, here you are,

ready to go to gaol, and you couldn't even think of a simple thing like that? Distribute the cows among the workers. They'll milk them and be able to feed their children. And later on you'll get your milkmaids."

"I never thought of that. I'll fix it...."

I went round the settlement with the director. I could see the construction work was being done badly. The houses were jerry-built, without any proper foundations. I gave him a piece of my mind. To be quite honest, I had already begun to distrust Kovalenko because of his perpetual repetition of that phrase: "I'll fix it...." I impressed upon him that I would come back and check up on everything. But when I visited the Stepnyak Farm again, I was astounded to find that almost nothing had changed! Supplies in the shop and the cafeteria were better, but that was due to the previous year's intervention. In other matters Kovalenko had not lifted a finger. The people were still having a bad time even with water, although on my last visit I had told the director to put a water-tank on a truck and let it deliver water to the houses—not much of a problem. But again in reply to every reprimand I heard the same phrase, "I'll fix it...."

Inefficiency there was, but instances of such, I would say, staggering helplessness and indifference were rare on the virgin lands. Functionaries who neglected their duties so disgracefully could not be tolerated and I had to point this out at the next plenary meeting of the Tselinograd Regional Party Committee. Provision of amenities means providing for people, consideration for them. It is always more than a purely economic task. Above all, it involves policy, and mistakes in this sphere are costly. For our mistakes we always pay heavily: at war, in lives; during peacetime, in material and moral resources.

To ensure a proper, full-blooded life in the area, the settlements in the steppe had to be in the charge of people who were not merely concerned with fulfilling the plan, but who felt a responsibility for everything that goes to make up people's lives. In Kokchetav Region, for instance, I liked visiting the Krasnoarmeyets Collective Farm. Not only because it was well managed, but because they also baked such wonderfully tasty bread. I don't think I have eaten better bread anywhere. It was so full-bodied and fragrant. It was particularly good in Pyotr Ivanovich Nikolayev's team. "When we're baking," he would say, "you can smell it a mile away!" I remember I once asked for a few loaves to treat the comrades in Alma-Ata and to teach the city's bakers how the job should be done.

When visiting the settlements, I would rejoice over every properly made well, every carefully planted sapling. I was delighted by the care that some home-loving people put into growing flowers and trees, and amazed at the indifference with which some others treated the appearance of their house, yard and the whole settlement.

I once spent the night in a village in the former Galkin District, Pavlodar Region (unfortunately, I have forgotten the name of the village and of the collective farm chairman with whom I stayed). In the morning I went out for a walk through the village and was rather surprised. It had only two streets, but along one there were trees in front of some of the houses, while the other street was completely bare. Why so? The chairman told me the following story.

This village had once been visited by the governor of Steppe Territory from the city of Omsk. Before the revolution all the present northern Kazakhstan steppes formed

part of this territory. During his visit the
governor ordered every family to plant as
many trees in front of their houses as there
were members in the family. Three years
later he revisited the village to see whether
his order had been obeyed. On inspection he
found that some houses had trees in front
of them while others were in the same bare
and dusty state as before. He then ordered
all the people living on the one street the
village then had to come out with their families and stand at the gates of their houses.
He handed a soldier a belt with a heavy
buckle and walked down the street. To the
householders who had planted trees he
said thank-you and gave a silver ruble. But
those who had neglected his command he
ordered to be thrashed with the belt—one
stroke for every missing tree. And while the
punishment was administered the governor
would shout, "Use the buckle, Vasily, the
buckle!"

"And that was how the trees appeared in
the streets," the chairman concluded, and
laughed.

Joking apart, one had to campaign real
hard for tree-planting on the new state farms
even in our day. And now, when I come to
the virgin lands and see the settlements

buried in greenery, the rustling shady parks,
the blossoming apple-trees and cherries, the
locust-trees and lilac, the tempting gleam
of innumerable ponds and reservoirs with
the inevitable anglers on the sun-scorched
banks–I recall with a smile the story of the
governor from Omsk.

*   *   *

I had to travel a lot, sometimes by train,
more often by air, and sometimes in the
course of one trip I used both. This combi-
nation saved a good deal of time, which was
always in short supply. During long stops
at junctions or regional centres, the carriage
served me as a hotel. A plane would be
waiting for me and in the course of a day
I would be able to make flying visits to
several districts or state farms.

An AN-2 had been specially fitted out for
me in Kiev. It carried a powerful radio-trans-
mitter and there were six seats in the pas-
sengers' compartment. The crew also carried a folding bed, which was kept in the
tail. In all other respects it was the same
reliable AN-2 work-horse that everyone
knows so well. For our travels it was indispensable. The pilots knew how to choose

a landing strip from the air and in the steppe they could land anywhere, beside any furrow, tractor or field camp.

Convenient though it was, this air-taxi service did wear you out. I had got used to it somehow, but one day our popular film-stars Lyubov Orlova, Marina Ladynina and Nikolai Kryuchkov had to go through it. They had come to entertain the virgin landers, but there was no audience: everyone was far away in the steppe. "We did a show in Kustanai," they complained to me, "but we want to see the virgin landers themselves. Can't you help us with some transport?"

"Well, why not? Here's my plane," I replied, and told the pilots, "Tomorrow I shall be busy in town and you will take these comrades round the work-teams. Wherever you see people, go in and land."

The pilots did their best. In one day they flew round two or perhaps even three districts. It was a windy day, the air pockets were fierce, and the actors came back to town feeling more dead than alive. Kryuchkov, being a tough character, was still firm on his feet but the women were worn out. I looked at them and reproached the pilot.

"It looks as if you've overdone it, Niko-lai?"

"But they insisted. When they got out of the plane, they lay down for a bit under the wing, then gave their show, and then it was 'Take us somewhere else'. Very courageous women...."

I thanked the actors but noticed that they no longer eyed my plane with the same envy as in the morning. There were some days when we had to spend hours circling over the steppe. One day the pilot said to me: "I think we can put you down as a pilot. You've got a hundred flying hours to your credit."

"What's the quota for pilots?"

"A hundred and twenty."

"Then it's too early for me to be a pilot."

"That depends. We're not doing normal flying."

"Isn't this normal?"

"What's our working altitude? A hundred metres. And how much hedge-hopping do we have to do to choose a landing strip? One hour counts as two in such conditions."

I liked the crew—captain Nikolai Moiseyev, second pilot Mubin Abishev, and flight engineer Alexander Kruglikov. Their little

plane, the "mosquito", as they called it, had
been in any number of adventures. In the
steppes, where there are not more than fifty
windless days in the year, this small aircraft
was always tossed about furiously. And
even on the ground it got no peace: on a
good many occasions loaded dump-trucks
had to be brought up to anchor the plane,
so that it would not be overturned and
smashed by the wind. It had to fly all the
year round, regardless of the weather and
sometimes breaking regulations. We landed
after sunset and even at night, which is categorically forbidden in the AN-2. But our
affairs had not been co-ordinated with the
regulations. My constant travelling compan-
ions, I realised, were past masters in their
profession.

In those days many airmen dreamed of
high speeds and long-distance flights, of jet
planes, and my pilots probably had similar
thoughts. But there was nothing for it. They
had other duties and they patiently and
honestly carried them out. Only once did
I see them extremely worried, almost scared.
It happened, if I am not mistaken, at the
Taman Division State Farm. We flew out
to a work-team in the far fields. It was May
and the grass was already a lush green. The

weather was clear and beneath us the steppe lay flat as a pancake. There was no difficulty about choosing a place to land. We landed, so it seemed to me, without any trouble. But as soon as the engine stopped, the first pilot, who usually left the plane after me, literally dashed for the exit with an abrupt "Excuse me. . . ."

I followed him out and saw him hurrying along the track left by our wheels in the grass. He was looking for something. Eventually he stopped, waved his arms and started shouting to the tractor drivers who were working nearby. A crowd gathered, I joined them and Moiseyev, pale and angry, said, "Look!"

In the grass half a metre away from the track of our left wheel lay a harrow, its teeth pointing skywards. From the air no one could have seen it and Moiseyev had noticed it only as the plane touched down. There could have been an unfortunate accident. I could hardly restrain the airmen, who were about to have a punch-up with the team-leader and the tractor drivers. Of course, they could not possibly have known that a plane was going to land on that particular field, but the harrow, like everything else when it was done with, ought to

have been put away and not just left lying there. It was an incident which clearly
showed that bad management and careless-
ness always stand on the borderline of
crime.

When I was leaving Kazakhstan and we
said good-bye, the captain of the plane told
me that in two years he had made 480 land-
ings with me in various parts of the steppe.
He said it with pride and I could understand his feelings as a professional.
Knowing the skill of this splendid pilot,
when I came to the virgin lands later as a
secretary of the CPSU Central Committee,
I flew only with Nikolai Grigoriyevich Moiseyev.

So once again our project was in full
swing, I was on the road all the time, slept
in snatches, ate what was going. And one
day in Tselinograd I suddenly felt ill. When
I came to, I was lying on a stretcher. Once
before this I had been taken from Semipalatinsk to Alma-Ata with a heart attack. I
had to rest up at home, fending off the doctors, who kept trying to get me into hospital. I used to joke my way out of it: once
you get hold of me, you'll keep me for good.
But the real point was that I had no time

to be ill. The virgin lands were piling up new projects and problems—difficult, sometimes muddled and always urgent.

The battle for grain had entered its decisive stage.

I should like to deal briefly with our agrotechnical policy on the virgin lands. Were there no mistakes at all in our work? No, I cannot say that. Did we know that we were venturing into a zone of particularly hazardous farming? Yes, we did, and we were prepared for it. Had we heard the warnings of experts that overall ploughing could turn the steppes into a desert? Of course, we had, and had taken them into account. The Party's agrotechnical policy on the virgin lands, to put it briefly, was to reduce to the minimum the negative effects of human intervention in the primeval nature of the steppe, to establish the best field cropping practices, and then to evolve a system of crop farming well adapted to the drought-threatened zone. But what this

would be in specific terms, we did not know
at first and could not have known. There
is a good oriental proverb that says,
"He who keeps walking will go all the
way."

Some time before the revolution Lenin
wrote:

"The Russian working class will win their
freedom and give an impetus to Europe by
their revolutionary action, full though it be
of errors—and let the philistines pride themselves on the infallibility of their revolutionary inaction."

Infallibility of inaction—an apt phrase! It
would have been the easiest thing in the
world to have left nature's larder untouched. That would have ruled out any possibility of error. But we came to these ancient
steppes with a profound belief in the power of human reason. We were convinced
that in the course of this huge project,
which was of such importance to the nation,
we should find a means of preserving the
fertility of the soil. And we sought this new
means from the outset.

We were fairly quick in abolishing pre-
seedtime spring ploughing. In the main we
had only May, June and autumn-ploughed
fallow, we introduced sowing of windbreak

rows, organised snow retention, made sure
to have a reliable fallow area, in short, we
did everything we could to solve the main
problem of farming in a drought-threatened
steppeland zone—retaining the moisture in
the soil. We also sorted out the sowing
schedule, although this was a by no means
simple problem. Today no one on the virgin lands sows before the second half of
May. This is now regarded as elementary.
But in those days.... "Sow in mud and
you'll be a lord!" was the old saying that
people repeated everywhere. And some experts also insisted on early sowing of the
virgin lands.

There were, however, other points of view,
and the experience of even the first year
showed that the fields sown in May yielded
a splendid crop. What was the reason—the
fresh vigour of the soil or the late sowing?
In 1955 late sowings were far more numerous and they obviously stood up better to
the drought. This seemed to clinch matters,
but the debate continued. It was particularly hard to convince the old-timers. At that
same Krasnoarmeyets Collective Farm, team
leader Nikolayev, who had treated me to
such tasty bread, ended our discussion of the
matter on the following note:

"We'll try, of course, but you can't imagine how hard it will be to hold back our men. As soon as they see they can get a harrow on the fields, they start sowing—at the double! That's what they're used to."

All the same, by the spring of 1956 in many of the new farms early sowing was regarded as something quite out of the ordinary, just as late sowing had been before. But the old habits still exerted a strong influence. The first secretary of the Yesil District Party Committee, Anatoly Rodionovich Nikulin, a splendid organiser, who became a Hero of Socialist Labour on the virgin lands, once told me in Moscow how one of the directors in his district nevertheless ignored the new sowing schedule.

"And who do you think it was who distinguished himself?" Nikulin named the state farm director. "We hadn't even celebrated May Day and suddenly in marches this 'champion': 'Comrade Secretary, the farm has finished its sowing!' And he makes a salute and clicks his heels. I nearly jumped out of my chair: 'You blunderer! Why did you hurry?' Because he wanted to be first in the district, he says. 'Well, you'll have no grain to show for it!' I told him."

And he didn't. The district harvested 16 centners per hectare on average, while the "pace-setter" produced only 6. It all happened a long time ago and after that incident the director had a fine work record, which is why I don't mention his name. But how ineradicable is the habit of reporting duty done and, of course, trying to be the first to do it, no matter if even grass won't grow there afterwards. And sometimes it won't.

But that is not the worst that can happen. Sometimes they do the ploughing well and sow according to schedule, but later, during harvesting, transportation, storage and processing lose nearly a third of the yield. Stopping waste is a major potential in farming today. Surely it is obvious that far less energy and funds are required to preserve what has been produced than to produce it. So pursuit of this aim has considerable advantages, corresponds to the Party's policy of raising efficiency, and, above all, serves the interests of the people.

I have special respect for people who calmly, without a lot of fuss or noise go ahead with their line in farming, always keeping the ultimate goal in sight. There were quite a few farming practices that had to be reconsidered on the virgin lands. For instance, it was just as important for us to know how deep to sow as when to sow. It was no accident, so it turned out, that Kokchetav Region stood up to the 1955 drought better than others. During a visit to the Zhdanov State Farm at sowing time I noticed that the seeds were being planted unusually deep. M. G. Roginets, the regional Party secretary, again explained "one little thing":

"Our agronomist maintains that seeds ought to be planted not at a depth of 3 or 4 centimetres, according to virgin land regulations, but at 6 or even 8 centimetres."

"They only sow maize that deep."

Unfortunately I don't remember the name of that agronomist, but I remember his explanation.

"You, see, Leonid Ilyich, I had experimental plots with plantings at that depth last year. There's no comparison! The secret is simple: the upper layer of soil quickly dries out in these parts and before the plant can put down roots the ground cracks and tears them apart. With our method the roots have a chance to develop properly and draw up the lower moisture, and by that time the rains come along to help them."

For two days I watched the new method of sowing. From the Zhdanov Farm that agronomist and I flew to the Chernigov Farm, then to other state farms. We re-adjusted the seed drills, crawled along the furrows and got hangnails on our fingers from poking the soil to test how deep the seeds were planted. And it was a fact that when the dry wind blew, the plantings on these farms stayed greener the longest— green islands amid the brown sun-scorched steppe. So it was a worthwhile idea. Now on the virgin lands, as distinct from other places, seeds are planted to a depth of eight centimetres. This has become an accepted technique.

So we gleaned experience, grain by grain. But fresh troubles lurked in the wake of success. The predictions of the experts about wind erosion began to come true. I remember how in Pavlodar Region together with district Party secretaries D. A. Asanov and I. F. Kaburneyev I saw the first tornadoes moving across the fields and the sand bank-ing up on the roads. It was a real "black storm" and you could hardly breathe. And soon after that the weeds appeared.

All this prompted me to go to Kurgan Re-gion, to see T. S. Maltsev at the Zavety Lenina Collective Farm. Terenty Semyonovich showed me some clean plantings of wheat without a single weed among them, then gave me his account of things. This man has a deep sense of conviction that stems from years of experience, folk wisdom and devotion to the soil. He spoke briefly, aphoristically.

"The mouldboard plough is the worst enemy of steppeland farming. My system is worth trying in your area. But may be you will think of something smarter, newer?"

"Reduce the amount of tillage to the minimum! Turn up the virgin soil, but then touch it as little as possible."

"Fallow—that's the main factor in steppeland cropping. You won't get grain if your virgin lands don't have fallow."

"Weeds taking a hold? That was to be expected. In some places they're already getting wheat mixed with wild oats. Later they'll be getting wild oats with some wheat in it. Some people got very upset. Wild oats, they say, are so hardy, what can we do about them? But a weed, you know, is a feeble thing. It's only hardy with the bad farmer. Yes, it's good that you're sowing later. You have to wait and lure the wild oats on, then destroy them. After that you can sow. It takes strong nerves. Field cropping is no job for weaklings."

I was much enlightened. But why, in that case, the reader will ask, did this useful know-how not spread speedily across the virgin lands? My answer is that the soil has a worse enemy than the plough and the weed, and this enemy is all kinds of imposed "recommendations". There have been too many of them and they have cost the country too much for us not to realise that for agriculture, because of its very nature, commands from above are contra-indicated. And although I must admit that I was sometimes very eager to "accelerate" and "step up" things, I restrained myself. People had to be given the chance to sort matters out for themselves, so that the know-how would evolve collectively.

Naturally I asked the journalists to publicise the achievements of the best state farms, I also organised seminars, and held conferences at the Central Committee. We gave high priority to developing a network of scientific institutions, getting them to study Soviet and world practices and find reliable ways of fighting soil erosion. I must mention the great work done by a team of scientists led by A. I. Barayev, now a Lenin Prize winner. I remember how insistently he advocated the importance of "small-scale irrigation"—letting the land lie fallow. And it was no accident that a soil-protective system of crop farming was subsequently devised precisely on the virgin lands of Kazakhstan.

We did all we could to defend the fallow and I have an interesting document to cite in this connection. A conference of specialists was being held in my office. It was June 9, 1955, at the very peak of the drought. The heat was terrible, the fields were burning, and we had to talk about the future—about the plan for the development of Kazakhstan's agriculture over the whole five-year period. Here is part of the minutes of that meeting which shows how the question was treated at that time:

Comrade Melnik (the republic's Minister of Agriculture): Now about crop rotation. In view of the introduction of millions of hectares of virgin lands we shall have to allocate a large amount of arable to fallow. For three years we have to sow wheat on wheat, and we shall do this, but in the fourth year we shall begin to let it lie fallow. If we allocate only one and a half million hec-

tares a year to fallow, as has been suggested, by 1960 we shall have introduced fallow on not more than one-sixth of all arable. From the agrotechnical point of view
this is very bad. Even if we find about another two million hectares of virgin land by
1960 to expand the arable, in our current
estimates for 1960 we shall still have to
somewhat reduce the amount of arable allotted to grain. This is the only way we can
ensure proper farming practices. And this
must be done at all costs. Otherwise we shall
ruin the soil in the first rotation.

Comrade Brezhnev: Does anyone contest
this?

Comrade Melnik: It is contested by the
decision of the Central Committee of the
Communist Party of Kazakhstan and the republic's Council of Ministers, which stipu-
lates a different figure for grain sowings. The
point is to change this previous decision because when it was calculated there was a
great deal that we could not yet accurately
allow for.

Comrade Brezhnev: Everything ought to
be more clearly stated on the subject of
fallow. I see we have reached something of
a deadlock. Is this connected with our decision?

Comrade Melnik: Yes, we are tied by it.

Comrade Brezhnev: We must work on the basis of economic efficiency. We need a serious and sober estimate dictated by the economic conditions. It already looks as if we must break into the zone of less moisture, of poorer quality land. I think it may be accepted conditionally that we shall find another couple of million hectares. But how about the total yield? Aren't you taking too much for fallow?

Comrade Melnik: No, we are not. Everything has been considered and agreed upon with the regions.

Comrade Arystanbekov (Deputy Minister of State Farms of the republic): We must bring the area of fallow up to between 16 and 18 per cent, then we shall be able to reach the targets that have been set.

Comrade Brezhnev: Still, how does this work out? If on average for the republic we have, say, 17 per cent fallow, shall we get the necessary total yield? Remember that with regard to total yield Kazakhstan is in a very special position. The Party and the government will be keeping a strict eye on that. We can't chop and change. We must have fallow, but how much? How much was there before we started on the virgin lands?

Comrade Andrianova (head of the scientific board of the republic's Ministry of Agriculture): In 1940 there was 18 per cent. For our zone, fallow is the foundation of crop farming. In addition, I want to mention perennial grass. I have in mind the zones threatened by wind erosion. In these zones we must adopt a longer crop rotation that includes grass as an anchor for the soil. This factor is not taken into account in the estimates. Besides the Maltsev crop rotation there must be rotations that include perennial grasses.

Comrade Brezhnev: The idea is all right. ... But what kind of lucerne will the Pavlodar people, for instance, have this year? They'll have neither grass, nor anchorage.

Comrade Andrianova: They are not doing anything about grass there, but they'll have to. Otherwise the erosion in that region will be worse than it's ever been anywhere. Wind erosion will become a terrible scourge for us if we don't start protecting ourselves against it now. These measures should be reflected in our plans and estimates for the five-year period.

Comrade Brezhnev: I agree with you. It is clear that our memorandum to the CPSU

Central Committee and the Government should state plainly that grain production in the republic will reach a certain level and stop there. This is quite understandable. In two years we shall open up 18 million hectares and we shall sow wheat on wheat for three years in succession, but it can't go on like that. The target we named tentatively earlier was an arbitrary figure, it was what we wanted to achieve. Subsequently we shall be able to reach the target by additions of large areas of virgin land, not by rapacious use of the soil.

Comrade Melnik: There isn't much time for drawing up the memorandum, only two or three days.

Comrade Brezhnev: Let the Central Committee secretary Fazyl Karibzhanovich Karibzhanov take charge of that. He will get you all together in his office and you can write it page by page day and night.

Comrade Melnik: That will mean closing down the ministry.

Comrade Brezhnev: This work is worth more than anything else. Make the memorandum short and readable. Only figures and conclusions. Don't complicate it, don't try to be subtle. Everything must be clear and precise.

The memorandum was drawn up and sent to Moscow. Time has shown that our estimates were correct.

In February 1956, at the 20th Congress of the CPSU I was proud to be able to report to the Party that the virgin lands project was a success. In two years the republic's sowing areas had been expanded to 27 million hectares. There were 23 million under grain, and of these 18 were under wheat—four times as much as before the project was launched. On behalf of all the virgin landers I assured the congress that Kazakhstan could produce a billion or more poods of grain per year.

But since I did not consider that everything had been done and completed, that all our difficulties were over, I stated further:

"The Kazakhstan Party organisation takes into account the fact that now when the republic's sowing areas are being brought up to 27 million hectares, our main potential for further increase of grain production lies in raising yields. In this sphere we still have many shortcomings. In connection with the opening up of the virgin lands it has become an urgent matter to work out a system of farm management providing for the local peculiarities of each collective or state farm in order to ensure the best use of the land and preserve soil fertility. This is a big proposition. We request the Academy of Sciences of the USSR, the Lenin All-Union Academy of Agricultural Sciences, and the Ministry of Agriculture and Ministry of State Farms of the USSR to help us so that the great work of developing the virgin lands may be brought to a successful conclusion."

In 1956 the great moment came for the virgin lands. A huge harvest was grown in the Kazakhstan steppes and instead of the promised 600 million poods the republic supplied the state with *one billion* poods. And I was truly happy when in that year Kazakhstan was awarded its first Order of Lenin for the first billion poods of virgin land grain. For that first billion, which secured the prestige of the virgin lands, a prestige that was never shaken either by the ravages of the elements or by the voluntarist decisions that intensified their effect.

Unfortunately, I was not able to see that gigantic harvest that had absorbed so much energy and effort. At the 20th Congress I was again elected secretary of the CPSU Central Committee.

That evening Kunayev, Satpayev, Zhurin,
Makarin and other Kazakhstan comrades
came to congratulate me at the Moskva
Hotel, where I was staying at the time. It
was a hurried, affectionate and somehow
wistful parting. They were anxious to get
home and I was thinking about my new
work. But I do want to say that it was sad
to bid good-bye to the friends, the steppe I
had grown to love, and the people, the virgin landers, who were so near and dear
to me.

Luckily, this parting proved to be not a very long one. The virgin lands, which formed such a precious and important period in my life, continued to excite and attract me. And after an interval taken up with other work, I turned to the virgin lands again. One of my many duties as General Secretary of the CPSU Central Committee was to support the soil-protective system of crop farming on the virgin lands evolved by Soviet scientists under A. I. Barayev. This system has now been introduced and it has protected the virgin lands from wind erosion. We were able to apply it in a very short space of time over a huge area, including other steppeland zones of the country, and thus reinforced the recommendations of science with the power of technology.

Even today I am constantly concerned with the virgin lands and often visit Kazakhstan. And I can say that I see there the actual realisation of my dream and the dream of hundreds of thousands of virgin landers.

Of course, by no means everything has been accomplished in the virgin steppes, the potential there is still enormous. But this is a subject apart. I want to speak of what has been achieved already, of things that are both heartening and impressive.

The virgin lands project in Kazakhstan was not only enormous but also economically profitable. I will cite figures to prove this. In the past 24 years Kazakhstan has sold the state more than 250 million tons of grain. In the same period, from 1954 to 1977 inclusive, total expenditure on the republic's agriculture—I stress, all its agriculture, not just the virgin lands—amounted to 21.1 billion rubles. And the turnover tax from the sale of grain in these years has yielded 27.2 billion rubles, that is to say, the country has made a clear profit of 6.1 billion rubles. Moreover, one must bear in mind that the fixed and working assets of the Kazakhstan collective and state farms today amount to 15 billion rubles. So all the work and all the expenditures have been recouped and produced a profit in the minimum amount of time. That is the splendid result of the most impressive battle for grain in the history of mankind! The ancient steppe proved to be a giant of strength. Transformed by human labour, it has brought stability to our whole agriculture and guaranteed a steady and adequate supply of grain. And this soil is still building up its potential.

Go for a flight across the vast expanses of the steppe. You will see not only cornfields, but the ribbons of macadamed road, settlements, railways, power transmission lines, elevators, industrial complexes, factories, and cities. It was the mighty grain of the former feather-grass lands that brought all this to life.

I remember, for example, what Akmolinsk was like when I first saw it. Low clay-walled houses, narrow streets, a mere 80,000 inhabitants.... But today? The city, now called Tselinograd (Virgin Land town), has three times as many people. It has been almost entirely rebuilt, redesigned. It has dozens of industrial enterprises, four institutes of higher education, fifteen technical colleges, which in the past three years alone have trained more than 20,000 specialists.

The virgin lands induced a mighty spurt in the development of Kazakhstan's productive forces, its economy, science and culture. Major industrial complexes have come into being, ninety new cities have sprung up, including the nationally famous Rudny, Ekibastuz, Yermak, Kentau, Arkalyk and Shevchenko. The republic is a producer of coal and oil, iron and steel, non-ferrous metals, mineral fertilisers, modern machine tools, machines and tractors. And no one is surprised that in once backward Kazakhstan a fast-neutron reactor has been put into operation.

Kazakhstan's star shines ever brighter in the constellation of the fraternal republics. Its development is measured in years and five-year periods, but it was all discussed, conceived, mulled over much earlier. Many features of the face that this land presents to the world today were charted nearly a quarter of a century ago, when my office at the Central Committee became more and more often a meeting place for scientists, prospectors, planning experts and designers. That also demanded much attention, time and effort.

Need I say how happy I am now with what I see: a gigantic agro-industrial complex has

taken shape in this area. It exerts a powerful influence on the economy of the whole
country. And the epic of the virgin lands has
once again shown the world the fine moral
qualities of Soviet people. It has become a
symbol of selfless service to the Homeland,
a great achievement of the socialist epoch.

Photographs

YCLers leaving for the virgin lands

Field camp site, May 1954

Leonid Brezhnev in the presidium
at a conference,
Kazakhstan, 1954

First furrow

Leonid Brezhnev at a virgin lands state farm

Cooking breakfast on outdoor stoves
at Slavyansky
State Farm

Settlement on the virgin lands

Virgin soil upturned

L. M. Kartauzov, Hero of Socialist Labour,
a virgin lands pioneer

Elevator ready for new harvest

Leonid Brezhnev, First Secretary,
Central Committee, Communist Party
of Kazakhstan

Bumper crop

At a grain-growing state farm

At a meeting on the 20th anniversary of the opening
up of the virgin and abandoned lands,
March 15, 1974

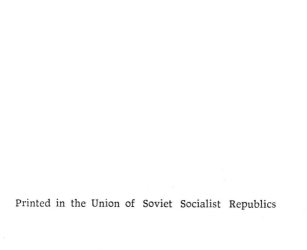

Printed in the Union of Soviet Socialist Republics